ITALY TRAVEL GUIDE

Unlocking the Dolce Vita. All the Things I wish I Knew Before Going to Italy for a Memorable Journey Through History, Culture, and Heavenly Cuisine

Giacomo Bonomio

Smart.Traveler Publishing

CONTENTS

INTRODUCTION

Welcome to Italy, a nation renowned for its art, architecture, history, and, of course, its mouthwatering cuisine. From the antiquated vestiges of Rome to the heartfelt channels of Venice, Italy brings something to the table for everybody. Italy is a destination you should not miss if you want to see the vibrant cities, unwind on the beaches, or hike through the stunning countryside.

We will give you all the information you need to plan your ideal Italian vacation in this travel guide. We'll cover everything from the best opportunity to visit, the top attractions to see, the most delectable food to try, and the most beautiful facilities to stay in. Therefore, kick back, unwind, and prepare to fall in love with Italy.

ITALY: AN ETERNAL HISTORY

Italy has a long and interesting history that dates back thousands of years. Since prehistoric times, people have lived on the Italian peninsula, which has been home to some of the world's most powerful and influential civilizations.

The antiquated Etruscans were one of the earliest civilizations to arise in Italy, around the eighth century BCE. They left behind a lot of literary, artistic, and architectural masterpieces as well as a sophisticated culture. The Romans eventually conquered the Etruscans and established one of history's greatest empires.

Italy became the center of the known world during the more than five centuries that the Roman Empire existed. Roman roads, aqueducts, and magnificent cities are still in use today. They likewise fostered a complex overall set of laws, a tremendous military, and a rich culture that has impacted craftsmanship, writing, and theory for a long time.

Italy was broken up into several smaller states and kingdoms after the Roman Empire fell. The Papal States in the center, the Byzantine Empire in the east, and several independent city-states like Venice, Florence, and Genoa were among these. Some of the greatest Renaissance artists and thinkers were born in these city-states, which were centers of art, commerce, and political intrigue.

Beginning in Italy in the 14th century, the Renaissance was a significant cultural and intellectual awakening that spread throughout Europe. It was marked by a new focus on humanism and the individual as well as a renewed interest in classical literature and art. Italians produced some of the Renaissance's greatest artists and thinkers, such as Galileo Galilei, Michelangelo, and Leonardo da Vinci.

Numerous foreign powers, including the French, the Spanish, and the Austrians, invaded Italy over the subsequent centuries. Despite this, Italy remained a hub for political and artistic turmoil. The rise of Italian nationalism and the unification of Italy as a single nation-state occurred in the 19th century.

Italy is still a cultural and economic powerhouse today. Its urban communities are home to a portion of the world's most prominent craftsmanship assortments, and its cooking and style are eminent all over the planet. People from all over the world continue to be inspired and influenced by Italy's rich history and cultural heritage, making it truly an eternal history.

CHAPTER 1: ROME

Rome, the capital of Italy, is one of the world's most historically significant cities. Due to its extensive and over two thousand years old cultural legacy, it is frequently referred to as the "Eternal City." Rome, which was established in 753 BC, is the location of some of the world's most recognizable buildings, including the Colosseum, the Pantheon, and the Roman Forum. Rome is a thriving, contemporary city that welcomes millions of visitors every year. Along with the city's vibrant culture, mouthwatering cuisine, and exciting nightlife, visitors can take advantage of the city's numerous museums, art galleries, and historical sites.

What to do in Rome

Rome is a charming city with a lot of history and culture. There are numerous things to see and do in the Eternal City, but the following are some of the most important ones to think about:

Check out the Colosseum
One of Rome's most well-known and frequently visited attractions is the Colosseum. It is an ancient amphitheater that was used for public spectacles like gladiatorial contests.

Visit the Roman Gathering
The Roman Forum was the hub of ancient Rome and is a massive ruin complex. Temple ruins, government structures and public spaces are all included.

Visit the Holy See
The Roman Catholic Church's headquarters are located in Vatican City, a sovereign city-state within Rome. It is where you'll find some

of the most famous works of art in the world, like Michelangelo's Sistine Chapel.

Toss a coin in the Trevi Wellspring
The Trevi Wellspring is a Florid show-stopper and a famous vacation spot. It is said that you will return to Rome if you throw a coin over your shoulder into the fountain.

Go to the Pantheon
The Pantheon is a previous Roman sanctuary and quite possibly of the best-protected old structure in the city. It is a stunning representation of Roman engineering and architecture.

Visit the Piazza Navona
The beautiful public square known as Piazza Navona is surrounded by fountains and Baroque structures. It is a famous spot for road entertainers and specialists.

Visit the museums in Capitoline
The Capitoline Galleries is a gathering of craftsmanship and archeological historical centers situated on the Capitoline Slope. They contain a huge assortment of old Roman relics and craftsmanship.

Try Roman food
Rome is known for its flavorful food, including pizza, pasta, and gelato, from there, the sky is the limit. Make sure to try some of the local specialties, like carbonara, suppl, and cacio e pepe.

Rome has a lot to offer, and these are just a few examples. Regardless of what your inclinations are, you make certain to track down something to appreciate in this lovely city.

Where to stay in Rome

There are many kinds of accommodation choices accessible in Rome, including hotels, lodgings, guesthouses, condos, and overnight boardinghouses. In each category, some popular options include:

Hotels:
The Spanish Steps Hotel: This is a small hotel that is close to the Spanish Steps and a designer shopping area.
Artemis Hotel: This is a contemporary hotel with a rooftop restaurant and spa near Termini Station.
St. George, Hotel Indigo: This is a spa-equipped luxury hotel with a rooftop terrace in the heart of Trastevere.

Hostels:
The Hostel in Yellow: A famous inn in the Monti neighborhood with an exuberant bar and dance club.
Hostel Alessandro Palace: This well-liked hostel provides a variety of private rooms with common bathrooms and dormitory-style rooms in addition to a rooftop patio with unobstructed city views. The hostel offers a bar, a common area with a TV and gaming consoles, and a shared kitchen where guests may prepare their meals, in addition to the rooftop terrace.
Trastevere Hotel: This is an affordable hostel in the trendy neighborhood of Trastevere.

Guesthouses:
Residenza Ruspoli Bonaparte: A posh guesthouse in a palace from the 16th century close to the Spanish Steps.
Roman Domus: A charming guesthouse with a terrace overlooking the Roman Forum in the Monti neighborhood.
Navona Exhibition and Nursery Suites: a small guest house with a garden courtyard close to Piazza Navona.

Apartments:

Monti Colosseum Patio: A contemporary apartment with a terrace that looks out over the Colosseum.

Domus Laurae: a large apartment with a private garden close to Vatican City.

Bright Apartment in Campo de Fiori: An apartment in the Campo de Fiori neighborhood that is bright and airy.

Hotels and inns:

The Light of the Angels: A warm and inviting bed and breakfast in the historic heart of Rome, close to the Colosseum and Roman Forum.

Residence of the Artist: A charming bed and breakfast in the city center, close to Piazza Navona and the Pantheon.

Rooms at B&B Roma Trastevere: This is an affordable little inn in the Trastevere area, with a housetop porch.

Where to eat in Rome

There are numerous excellent restaurants to choose from in Rome, which is known for its mouthwatering Italian cuisine. Here are some suggestions:

Da Enzo al 29

This trattoria is situated in the Trastevere area and is well known for its natively constructed pasta dishes. Be sure to make a reservation because it's a popular spot.

Pizza joint La Montecarlo

For an exemplary pizza experience, go to this pizza shop close to the Colosseum. The toppings are delicious and the dough is made with natural yeast.

Roscioli

Roscioli is a gourmet emporium and restaurant that is well-known for its outstanding selection of wine, cheese, and cured meats. The establishment is owned and run by the Roscioli family and you can enjoy a posh lunch.

Da Danilo

Traditional Roman dishes like carbonara and cacio e pepe can be found at Danilo's Restaurant, another excellent option in Trastevere. Both the prices and the portions are generous.

Osteria del Pegno

Near the Pantheon is the Michelin-starred Osteria del Pegno, which serves innovative interpretations of traditional Italian fare. It's a piece on the costly side, yet worth the effort for a unique event.

Rome has many wonderful restaurants, and these are just a few of them. While you're there, don't forget to try espresso and gelato!

What to bring home from Rome

Rome offers different keepsakes and gifts that you can bring back home as a token of your excursion. Some popular choices are as follows:

Leather goods

Rome is home to a plethora of leather goods shops, including wallets, belts, jackets, and bags. Italy is known for its high-quality leather.

Roman Wine

Rome is home to numerous wineries and shops where you can purchase a bottle of Italian wine—Italy is one of the world's largest wine producers.

Roman cuisine

Pasta, olive oil, truffles, and cheese, among other delectable Italian fare, can be brought back from your trip.

Vatican Gifts

Visitors can purchase a variety of religious and cultural items in Vatican City. Rosaries, postcards and prints, religious artifacts, Vatican coins and stamps, books, and trinkets are some of the most popular presents.

Fashion

Rome is a center point of Italian style, and you can purchase dresses, shoes, and embellishments from numerous renowned Italian creators.

Antiquity from Rome

Rome has a rich history, and you can find many secondhand shops and stores selling Roman coins, figures, and different curios.

Ceramics
Italy's ceramics are world-renowned, and you can buy exquisite plates, bowls, and other kitchenware there.

Craftsmanship
You can buy paintings, sculptures, and other works of art from local artists in Rome's numerous art galleries.

Roman Sweets
You can bring back a box of Italy's delicious chocolates as a sweet memento of your trip.

Roman Coffee
You can bring back some Italian espresso or a coffee machine to have a taste of Italy at home, as Italy is known for its coffee.

CHAPTER 2: MILAN

The energetic and multicultural city of Milan is situated in northern Italy. It is the second-largest city in Italy and is largely regarded as the global center of fashion and design. Milan is renowned for its rich history and cultural legacy. The city is renowned for its cutting-edge architecture and design, with structures like the Pirelli Tower and the Unicredit Tower. The city is also well-known for its cuisine, with many classic Italian dishes like panettone and risotto alla Milanese having their origins in Milan. Milan is a must-visit location for tourists from across the world since it has something to offer everyone, whether they are interested in fashion, art, design, history, or food.

Milan is a clamoring city in northern Italy and is known for its style, craftsmanship, and rich history. Some suggestions for things to do in Milan are as follows:

Go to the Duomo
One of the city's most popular tourist attractions is the stunning Milan Cathedral, also known as the Duomo. Climbers can get a great view of Milan from the top.

Check the Da Vinci's "The Last Supper"
Situated in the congregation of St Nick Maria delle Grazie, Da Vinci's Last Dinner is one of the world's most popular works of art. Make

certain to book your tickets ahead of time, as they frequently sell out.

Explore the Vittorio Emanuele II Galleria
This breathtaking glass-shrouded arcade is home to top-of-the-line shops, bistros, and cafés. While you're there, don't forget to take a look up at the stunning ceiling.

Take a tour of Brera
Art galleries, charming cafes, and boutiques abound in this trendy neighborhood. A great spot to spend an afternoon is here.

Visit Sforza Palace
Some of Milan's most important art collections are housed in this medieval fortress-turned museum, including works by Michelangelo and Leonardo da Vinci.

Navigli District Canals
The Naviglio Grande and the Naviglio Pavese are the two main canals that make up the Navigli, and other smaller canals join them. A lively and inviting ambiance is created by the canals' colorful buildings, cafes, restaurants, and shops. Although the canals were once used to move supplies throughout the city, they are now primarily used for leisure activities like dining, shopping, and sightseeing.

Shop at Quadrilatero d'Oro
This region, also known as the "Golden Quadrilateral," is named after the city's four principal streets, Via Monte Napoleone, Via Alessandro Manzoni, Via della Spiga, and Corso Venezia, which are home to some of the most exclusive fashion brands in the world. Even if you don't want to buy designer clothes, the beautiful window displays are worth a visit.

Go to a soccer game

AC Milan and Inter Milan, two of Italy's most well-known soccer teams, are based in Milan. It is a must to attend a soccer game at the San Siro stadium.

Go for a road trip

Milan is situated in the Lombardy locale, which is known for its lovely lakes, like Lake Como and Lake Garda. A great way to get away from the city and take in some natural beauty is to take a day trip to one of these picturesque locations.

Where to stay in Milan

Milan offers an extensive variety of accommodation choices, from affordable well-disposed inns to lavish five-star lodgings. Some suggestions are as follows:

Hotels

Milan has a large number of hotels to browse, to suit your budget and needs for extravagance. The Hotel Principe di Savoia, the Grand Hotel et de Milan, and the Bulgari Hotel Milan are among the city's most well-liked accommodations.

Hostels

Assuming you're searching for more reasonable accommodation, Milan has a few inns that offer beautiful residence-style rooms or confidential rooms. The Queen Hostel Milan, MEININGER Milano Garibaldi, and Ostello Bello Grande are among the city's most well-liked hostels.

Apartments

On the off chance that you lean toward a usual hangout spot insight, leasing a loft in Milan might be a decent choice for you. With a kitchen and other amenities, many apartments are available for short-term rentals. Apartments can be found on websites like Airbnb and HomeAway.

Overnight boardinghouses
A bed and breakfast is another option for cheap lodging. There are several B&Bs all over Milan, offering a more intimate stay and the chance to meet the locals.

Guesthouses
If you're looking for a more intimate and local experience, guesthouses are another option. Milan's guesthouses range in size from modest establishments run by a single family to more substantial establishments with multiple rooms.

Overall, your preferences, travel plans, and budget will all play a role in determining the best lodging option for you. It's really smart to explore various choices and read audits from past visitors to assist you with settling on an educated choice.

Where to eat in Milan

Milan is a city known for its lively food scene, with a wide assortment of culinary choices to suit all preferences and budgets. Milan's dining options include the following:

Trattoria Milanese
This conventional Milanese café is known for its flavorful risotto alla Milanese and cotoletta alla Milanese. It is situated in the heart of Milan and has a warm and inviting environment.

Luini Panzerotti
This is a popular bakery situated in the center of Milan. They serve panzerotti, which is similar to a calzone or a fried turnover. It's an ideal choice for a speedy and delicious lunch.

The Paper Moon

This stylish and rich eatery is situated in the core of Milan and serves tasty Italian food. It's a great spot for a romantic dinner or a special occasion.

Ratanà

Local and seasonal ingredients are used in this restaurant's innovative take on traditional Italian cuisine. The café is situated in the trendy Isola area.

Taglio

This is a famous pizza shop that serves customary Neapolitan-style pizza. Additionally, they have an excellent selection of wines and craft beers.

Brellin El

This comfortable and rural eatery serves conventional Milanese cooking. It has a charming seating area outside and is in the Navigli district.

Food Court at La Rinascente

This high-end food hall on the top floor of the La Rinascente department store serves a wide range of gourmet Italian fare, including seafood, pizza, and pasta.

Milan has a lot of great places to eat, and these are just a few of them. Whether you're looking for classic Italian fare or something more cutting-edge and contemporary, there's something here for everyone.

What to bring home from Milan

Because of its high-end fashion and design, Milan is a popular destination for souvenir shopping.

Designer Fashion

You might want to think about bringing home a piece of clothing, a bag, or a pair of shoes from one of Prada, Gucci, or Armani's world-class designer stores while you are in Milan.

Vino Italiano

Milan is home to numerous wine shops where you can pick up a bottle of your favorite wine. Italy is known for its wine.

Italian Food Items

You might want to think about bringing home some Italian food products like olive oil, pasta, or cheese because Milan is known for its delicious cuisine.

Italian pastries

You can purchase Italian sweets like panettone, cannoli, and tiramisu at many pastry shops in Milan.

Craftsmanship

Additionally, Milan is well-known for its handmade goods, such as jewelry, ceramics, and leather goods. These one-of-a-kind items make excellent gifts and keepsakes.

Milanese Memorabilia

To bring back something exceptionally Milanese, consider buying memorabilia, for example, a smaller-than-usual copy of the Duomo di Milano, a banner of a well-known painting in the Pinacoteca di Brera, or a scarf with the city's crest.

CHAPTER 3: FLORENCE

The lovely and historic city of Florence, also known as Firenze in Italian, is situated in the Tuscany region of central Italy. Both art lovers and history buffs like visiting the city because of its famed Renaissance artwork and architecture. Many influential artists and thinkers, including Michelangelo, Leonardo da Vinci, and Galileo Galilei, were born and raised in Florence, which is credited as the birthplace of the Italian Renaissance. Some of the most well-known works of art in the world, such as Botticelli's Birth of Venus and Michelangelo's David statue, may be found in the city. Florence is a must-visit, and it will make an impression, whether you're interested in art, architecture, history, or simply want to take in the atmosphere of a stunning Italian city.

Florence, situated in the core of Tuscany, Italy, is a delightful city that is well known for its specialty, culture, history, and design. There are numerous things to see and do in Florence, including:

You can go to the Uffizi Gallery
One of the world's most well-known museums of art is the Uffizi Gallery, which houses Renaissance masterpieces by Michelangelo, Botticelli, and Leonardo da Vinci.

See David by Michelangelo
The Accademia Exhibition is home to Michelangelo's David, quite possibly of the most renowned model on the planet. In addition, the gallery features other works by Renaissance artists and Michelangelo.

Ascend the Duomo
The stunning dome of the Florence Cathedral, also known as the Duomo, was designed by Filippo Brunelleschi. For a stunning view of the city, visitors can ascend the dome.

Boboli Gardens
The Boboli Nurseries is a lovely park situated behind the Pitti palace. The gardens have beautiful views of the city, fountains, and sculptures for visitors to enjoy.

Take a trip to Palazzo Vecchio
The Palazzo Vecchio, a medieval palace in Florence, has served as the political hub for centuries. Guests can Visit the royal residence and see the dazzling frescoes that brighten its walls.

Stroll across the Ponte Vecchio

The Arno River is crossed by the famous Ponte Vecchio bridge. The scaffold is fixed with shops selling adornments, cowhide merchandise, and trinkets.

Try the Tuscany Food
The dishes known as ribollita (a vegetable soup), bistecca alla Fiorentina (a thick, juicy steak), and pappa al pomodoro (a bread and tomato soup) are among Florence's most famous Tuscan dishes.

Road trip to the Tuscan open country
Florence is situated in the core of Tuscany, which is known for its lovely open country and pleasant towns. A day trip to San Gimignano, Siena, or the Chianti wine region is an option for visitors.

Where to stay in Florence

There are a lot of places to stay in Florence, which is a popular tourist destination in Italy. There are a few choices:

Hotels
The best hotels include the Inn Bernini Royal Residence, the Four Seasons Inn Firenze, and the Inn Lungarno.

B&Bs
Florence's Bed and Breakfasts (B&Bs) are a popular choice because they offer a more personal and cozy stay. Some exceptionally ranked B&Bs include Il Bargello Bed and Breakfast, La Dimora degli Angeli, and Antica Torre di Via Tornabuoni 1.

Apartments
If you want more privacy and space, renting an apartment can be a good choice. Airbnb, HomeAway, and VRBO are a few well-known websites for renting apartments.

Hostels

Florence has a lot of hostels, which are a good option for travelers on a tight budget. Some profoundly appraised inns include the Plus Florence, the Academy Hostel, and the Ostello Tasso.

There are numerous excellent restaurants to choose from in Florence, Italy, which is known for its mouthwatering Italian cuisine. Florence's best restaurants include the following:

Osteria del Cinghiale Bianco

This conventional Tuscan eatery works in game dishes like wild pigs and offers a comfortable and natural climate.

Trattoria Mario

This traditional trattoria is a favorite among locals because it serves authentic Italian food at reasonable prices.

La Giostra

Situated in an enchanting middle age tower, La Giostra offers an upscale eating experience.

Il Santo Bevitore

Il Santo Bevitore is a trendy and contemporary restaurant that serves a variety of Italian dishes using organic and seasonal ingredients.

All'Antico Vinaio

Foodies looking for authentic Tuscan street food, including the well-known "schiacciata" sandwiches, should visit All'Antico Vinaio, a casual and bustling sandwich shop.

Procacci

Procacci is an excellent option for a light lunch because of its truffle sandwiches and extensive wine list.

Il Latini

Il Latini is known for its hearty Florentine steak and traditional Tuscan cuisine. It is a historic restaurant with a lively and welcoming atmosphere.

Ristorante Il Palagio

Il Palagio is a restaurant inside the opulent Four Seasons Hotel that serves contemporary fine dining using local and fresh ingredients.

In Florence, there are a plethora of excellent restaurants to choose from. Bon appétit!

What to bring home from Florence

Florence is famous for its beautiful art, architecture, and fashion. As a result, the city has many interesting and one-of-a-kind souvenirs. Some ideas are as follows:

Leather articles

Florence is popular for its top-notch cowhide items, including coats, packs, belts, and wallets.

Paper goods made by artisans

Beautiful notebooks, journals, and other paper goods can be found in many artisanal paper shops in Florence.

Florentine pottery

Ceramics with hand-painted designs, such as plates, bowls, and other decorative items, can be found in numerous shops throughout Florence.

Olive oil and wine

There are numerous vineyards and olive groves around Florence where you can sample and purchase Tuscany's excellent wines and olive oils.

Clothing Accessories

You can find high-end accessories like scarves, ties, and sunglasses in Florence because it is home to many luxury fashion brands like Gucci and Salvatore Ferragamo.

Food specialties

Tuscan cooking is renowned for its generous meat dishes and restored meats like prosciutto, as well as its cheeses like pecorino and Parmigiano-Reggiano.

Gold jewelry from Florencia

Goldsmithing has a long history in Florence, and beautiful gold jewelry can be found in a lot of shops all over the city.

Religious artifacts

Florence is a memorable focal point of the Catholic Church, and you can find numerous religious things like rosaries and crosses around the city.

Northeastern Italy is home to one of the most well-liked tourist attractions in the world; Venice, or Venezia as it is known in Italian. It is renowned for its charming canals, passionate gondola rides, and gorgeous architecture. Venice is made up of a network of interconnected islands connected by bridges and canals. Tourists can explore its hidden courtyards and secret gardens by meandering through its tinier streets and across its twisting bridges. Venice is a must-visit destination that will provide you with priceless memories, regardless of whether you have an interest in history, art, or architecture, or simply want to feel the special ambiance of this magnificent city.

What to do in Venice

The historic and beautiful city of Venice has a lot to offer visitors in the way of activities and sights. The following are some of Venice's most popular activities:

Ride in a gondola
A gondola ride is a must-do activity in Venice. Glide through the canals to get a different look at the city.

Square of St. Mark's
You can take in the stunning St. Mark's Basilica and the Doge's Palace when you go to the well-known St. Mark's Square.

Bridge of Rialto
The Rialto Extension is quite possibly Venice's most famous milestone. Cross the scaffold and Visit the Rialto Market, where you can test nearby food and drink.

Islands of Murano and Burano
Take a boat ride to the nearby islands of Murano and Burano to observe traditional techniques for lacemaking and glass blowing.

Collection of Peggy Guggenheim
For art enthusiasts, the Peggy Guggenheim Collection is a must-see collection of works by some of the most important artists of the 20th century.

Galleries of the Academy
The impressive Gallerie dell'Accademia collection of Venetian art, which includes works by Bellini, Titian, and Veronese, is another must-see museum.

Biennale of Venice
Every two years, Venice, Italy hosts the Biennale of Venice, a significant exhibition of contemporary art. It was originally held in 1895 and has since grown to be of the most significant cultural occasions worldwide. The Biennale unites artists, curators, collectors, and art aficionados from all over the world and

showcases a variety of art disciplines, including painting, sculpture, installation, video, and performance art.

Lose yourself in the crowds
Venice was designed to be explored on foot. Explore the city's hidden corners, get lost in its narrow streets and alleys, and enjoy its distinctive charm.

Try the local delicacies
Cicchetti, cuttlefish ink pasta, and spritz cocktails are just a few of the local delicacies to try in Venice, which is known for its delicious cuisine.

Go to a theatre or opera
Venice has a rich cultural history, and the city regularly hosts theater, classical music, and opera performances.

These are just a few suggestions to get you started; depending on your interests and preferences, there are many more things to see and do in Venice.

Where to stay in Venice

From extravagant hotels to budget-friendly guesthouses and hostels, Venice has a variety of lodging options to suit a variety of preferences and budgets. The following are some choices to think about:

Hotels
The famous Gritti Palace and the Belmond Hotel Cipriani are two of the many opulent hotels in Venice. Additionally, numerous mid-range hotels provide hospitable lodging at cost-effective rates. The Hotel Danieli, the Hotel Londra Palace, and the Hotel Al Ponte Antico are among the most well-known hotels in Venice.

B&Bs and guesthouses

There are many bed and breakfasts and guesthouses in Venice that are more intimate than hotels. Ca' San Giorgio, Ca' Angeli, and Ca' dei Dogi are a few popular choices.

Hostels

Hostels can be a great option for budget travelers. Generator Venice, Ostello Santa Fosca, and Venice Fish Hostel are among the city's most well-liked hostels.

Rental Apartments

Venice additionally offers many getaway rentals, including lofts and houses. If you're traveling with a group or want more space and privacy, these might be a good choice for you. Airbnb, HomeAway, and VRBO are a few well-known websites for vacation rental properties.

Because Venice is a popular tourist destination, it is essential to reserve your lodging well in advance, especially during peak travel times.

Where to eat in Venice

There are numerous dining options in Venice, which has a thriving culinary scene. Here are a few suggestions for spots to eat in Venice:

The Fiore Osteria

This Michelin-starred restaurant is known for its inventive Venetian cuisine made with local Rialto market-sourced fresh ingredients. The restaurant is ideal for a special occasion because of its warm and sophisticated atmosphere.

Trattoria alla Madonna

This conventional Venetian eatery has been presenting exemplary dishes for more than 50 years. The seafood and pasta dishes on the menu are all made with fresh, local ingredients.

Squero's Osteria

This cozy restaurant in the Dorsoduro area is known for its delicious Cicchetti, or small plates, and other traditional Venetian dishes. The café has an incredible atmosphere, with seating outside ignoring the channel.

Ristorante Quadri

Ristorante Quadri, which is in St. Mark's Square, has stunning views of the square and the basilica. The eatery's menu highlights contemporary Italian cooking with an emphasis on fish.

Risorto Bacaro

In the Cannaregio neighborhood, this charming wine bar is a popular destination for locals. The menu includes a scope of cicchetti and little plates, as well as an extraordinary choice of neighborhood wines.

What to bring home from Venice

Venice is famous for its art, history, and culture, and you can bring back a few things as gifts or souvenirs from your trip. Here are a few concepts:

Glass from Venice
Venice's hand-blown glass, which has been made on the island of Murano for centuries, is what makes the city famous. Vases, bowls, and jewelry are among the many types of glassware available.

Masks
Venetians are well-known for their vibrant masks, which are typically donned during Carnival. The designs of these masks range from simple and refined to elaborate and theatrical.

Lace of Burano
The intricate lacework of Burano, an island in the Venetian lagoon, is well-known. Burano lace can be found in a variety of products, including tablecloths, doilies, and clothing.

Venetian Food and Wine
Prosecco wine, olive oil, and Venetian biscuits are just a few of the local delicacies you can take home from Venice's rich culinary heritage.

Artwork
Venice has a long history of art, and you can find everything from old oil paintings to modern art in galleries and markets all over the city.

Gondolier Caps
You can purchase a gondolier hat, the traditional hat worn by the city's famous gondoliers, for a quirky souvenir.

Printed in Venice

Venetian paper is used in a variety of notebooks, journals, and other paper goods because the city has a long tradition of producing high-quality paper.

Venetian Fragrance

Venice has a long tradition of perfume production, and a variety of scents are influenced by the city's distinctive atmosphere and history.

Overall, there are a lot of options, so you're sure to find something that meets your preferences and your budget.

Italy's northern region is home to the picturesque and ancient city of Verona. The location of William Shakespeare's tragic love romance "Romeo and Juliet" has made the city famous and earned it the moniker "city of love." It's understandable why Verona's historic center is included as a UNESCO World Heritage Site. The Verona Arena, a beautifully preserved Roman amphitheater, and the Piazza delle Erbe, a bustling center with vibrant markets and cafes, are just two of the numerous historic structures and sites that visitors can explore. The Basilica di San Zeno Maggiore, with its lovely Romanesque architecture, and the Castelvecchio Museum, which houses an amazing collection of medieval and Renaissance art, are just two of the spectacular churches and art galleries that can also be found in Verona.

What to do in Verona

Verona is a beautiful city in northern Italy with a long history and culture. Verona has a lot to offer, including the following:

Casa di Giulietta

The balcony where Romeo is said to have wooed Juliet can be seen when you visit Juliet's house, Casa di Giulietta. The patio likewise has a bronze sculpture of Juliet, which guests can contact for good karma.

Piazza delle Erbe

Take a look around the lively Piazza delle Erbe, which was once the site of a Roman forum. Here, you can buy souvenirs, fresh produce, and other goods from vendors.

Arena di Verona

Visit the Roman amphitheater known as the Arena di Verona, which is still used for opera and concert performances today.

Verona's Adige River

Take a stroll along Verona's Adige River, which winds its way through the city center. You can take in the city and the stunning scenery at the same time.

Romanesque Basilica di San Zeno Maggiore

Take a tour of the stunning Romanesque Basilica di San Zeno Maggiore, which was built in the 12th century. Saint Zeno, Verona's patron saint, is honored in the church's dedication.

Castelvecchio Museum

The Castelvecchio Museum has art from the Middle Ages and the Renaissance, as well as weapons and armor.

Giusti Nurseries

Visit the Giusti Nurseries, a wonderful Renaissance garden with wellsprings, sculptures, and a labyrinth.

Verona's historic center

Take a stroll through Verona's UNESCO World Heritage-listed historic center. Beautiful palaces, churches, and other structures from the 16th century are on display.

Verona Opera Festival
Participate in the Verona Opera Festival, which takes place each summer in the Arena di Verona. It is one of the world's most well-known opera festivals.

Where to stay in Verona

Verona offers various facilities to suit various budgets and inclinations. There are a few choices:

Inns
Verona has numerous inns like Hotel Accademia, Hotel Milano & SPA, Hotel Mastino, and Hotel Verona.

B&Bs
B&B all'Opera, B&B Carmen, and B&B Al Filarmonico are among the most well-liked examples.

Apartments
Renting an apartment in Verona might be a good choice if you want more space and privacy. On well-known booking sites like Airbnb, Booking.com, and Expedia, a lot of apartments are for rent.

Hostels
Verona also has several hostels that provide budget-friendly lodging for tourists. Ostello della Gioventu Verona and Arena Hostel Verona are two well-known choices.

Agriturismi
For a more extraordinary encounter, you can consider remaining in an agriturismo, which is a homestead that offers accommodation to

visitors. In the vicinity of Verona, several agriturismi provide a glimpse into rural life.

It's essential to book your accommodation ahead of time, particularly during the peak season or on the other hand on the off chance that you're visiting during a famous occasion like the Verona Opera Celebration.

Where to eat in Verona

Verona is known for its delectable Italian food and offers various eating choices to suit various budgets and tastes. Verona has the following dining options:

Trattoria al Pompiere
This eatery is situated in a noteworthy structure and serves conventional Veronese dishes like risotto all'Amarone and gnocchi di zucca.

Osteria del Bugiardo
Osteria del Bugiardo is renowned for its inventive takes on traditional Italian dishes. It also has a great selection of wines from the area.

Antica Bottega del Vino
This is an intimate wine bar and restaurant that serves delectable Italian cuisine. Additionally, it is well-known for its extensive wine list.

La Taverna di Via Stella
This restaurant serves delicious seafood and other Italian specialties. Additionally, it has a fantastic wine selection.

Locanda 4 Cuochi

This eatery has a cutting-edge and trendy stylistic theme and serves innovative Italian food made with new, occasional fixings.

Pizza joint da Michele
This pizza shop is known for its delightful Neapolitan-style pizza. Be prepared to wait in line because this is a popular spot.

Gelateria Ponte Pietra
This gelateria offers a selection of flavorful homemade gelato.

Caffè Monte Baldo
This café serves delectable pastries and coffee. It's an extraordinary spot to human watch and take in the energetic air.

These are only a couple of the numerous extraordinary eateries and bistros in Verona. It's additionally worth investigating the nearby business sectors and attempting a portion of the new produce and neighborhood claims to fame.

What to bring home from Verona

In Verona, Italy, you can buy a lot of things to take back with you. A few suggestions are as follows:

Wine
Valpolicella, Amarone, and Soave are examples of high-quality wines that Verona is known for producing. You can bring back a container or two as a gift.

Olive oil
Italy is additionally known for delivering phenomenal olive oil, and Verona is no exemption. Find an extra-virgin olive oil bottle to take home.

Handicrafts

There are a lot of artisans in Verona who make beautiful handicrafts, like ceramics, leather goods, and lace. These things are available at markets and shops all over the city.

Chocolate
Verona has a long history of making chocolate, and there are many different kinds to choose from to take home as a memento. "Tortellini di cioccolato," a local delicacy, can be found in chocolate shops.

Opera Souvenirs
Verona is well-known for its Opera Festival, which takes place in the Arena di Verona. CDs, DVDs, and posters are just a few of the festival-related souvenirs you can find.

Verona-themed things
You can track down numerous things that highlight the images of Verona, for example, the Juliet overhang, the Field di Verona, and the city's escutcheon. Look for these symbols on magnets, keychains, and t-shirts.

CHAPTER 6: GENOA

The historic port city of Genoa, also known as Genova in Italian, is situated in the country's northwest. Christopher Columbus was born in this city, which is also well-known for its maritime heritage. Genoa is also renowned for its delectable culinary specialties including focaccia, pesto, and fresh seafood with several food markets and kiosks dominating the street food scene. Genoa is also a lively and energetic city with a bustling port district and a lively nightlife scene. The picturesque waterfront, the numerous stores and boutiques in the city center, and the many parks and gardens are all options for visitors to enjoy.

What to do in Genoa

On Italy's northwest coast, is a stunning and historic port city called Genoa. In Genoa, there are a few things to do:

Take in the historic district
Genoa's notable community, a UNESCO World Legacy Site, is a labyrinth of thin roads, old structures, and enchanting piazzas. Visit the House of God of San Lorenzo, the Palazzo Ducale, and the Piazza de Ferrari.

Check out the Aquarium
With over 15,000 animals from 400 species, the Genoa Aquarium is one of the largest and most impressive in Europe. It's a great place to take kids or anyone who wants to learn more about marine life.

Take a walk along the coast
Shops, restaurants, and cafes line the city's seafront promenade, making it a popular destination for both locals and visitors. Rent a bike, go for a walk, or stop for ice cream.

Try some of the local food
Pesto alla Genovese, focaccia, and farinata are just a few of Genoa's famous dishes. Make a beeline for the Mercato Orientale or one of the numerous trattorias in the city to test the nearby charge.

Visit the Palazzi dei Rolli
The Palazzi dei Rolli is an assortment of 42 castles in Genoa that were once used to have significant visitors. They are a demonstration of the city's riches and influence during the Renaissance and Florid periods, and many are currently open to people in general.

Go for a day trip
The Ligurian coast can be easily explored from Genoa. Take a train to the charming towns of Cinque Terre and Portofino, or travel inland to the stunning Langhe region's countryside.

Take a funicular ride
Numerous funiculars in Genoa provide breathtaking views of the city and the sea. The Funicolare Zecca Righi is the most well-known one. It takes you to the top of the Righi Hill, where you can get a great view of the city and the surrounding area.

Where to stay in Genoa

If you're looking for a place to stay in Genoa, you can choose from a wide range of options based on your preferences and budget. Some suggestions are as follows:

Hotels
Genoa is home to numerous luxury and budget-friendly hotels. The Grand Hotel Savoia, NH Collection Genova Marina, and Hotel Bristol Palace are a few of Genoa's most well-known hotels.

Hostels

Genoa has various lodgings that are reasonable and famous among explorers and voyagers on a budget. The Mini Hotel, Generator Hostel Genoa, and the Olympia Hostel are a few of the recommended hostels.

Apartments
Assuming that you like to have your own space, you can search for lofts on sites like Airbnb, Booking.com, or HomeAway. These websites offer everything from cheap apartments to expensive penthouses.

Inns and B&Bs
In Genoa, bed and breakfasts are a popular choice because they offer a more intimate experience. The B&B Domitilla, B&B Quarto Piano, and B&B Le 4 Stagioni are three of Genoa's most well-known bed and breakfasts.

It is advisable to book in advance, regardless of the type of lodging you select, particularly during peak travel times.

Where to eat in Genoa

Genoa is known for its tasty cooking, which includes fish, pesto, focaccia, and farinata. Genoa's dining options include the following:

Trattoria Rosmarino
This is a cozy restaurant in Genoa's historic center that serves up traditional Ligurian fare like fish soup and pasta with pesto.

Antica Osteria di Vico Palla
This is a rustic and welcoming restaurant that serves traditional Genoa cuisine, such as stuffed squid and pansoti with walnut sauce.

La Superba

A cutting-edge and exquisite eatery that offers contemporary turns on exemplary Ligurian dishes, for example, octopus carpaccio and risotto with zucchini blossoms.

Il Marin
Fresh fish dishes and stunning views of the sea can be found at Il Marin, a seafood restaurant in Boccadasse's charming neighborhood.

Pizzeria Capolinea
This is a well-known pizzeria that serves authentic Neapolitan-style pizza as well as other Italian delicacies like lasagna and cannelloni.

Focacceria di San Francesco
This is a historic bakery that makes some of Genoa's best focaccia, as well as farinata and cecina, and other Ligurian specialties.

Osteria della Corte
A conventional trattoria situated in the core of the city, offering a wide choice of Ligurian dishes and wines.

These are only a couple of the numerous extraordinary cafés in Genoa, and there are a lot of other unlikely treasures ready to be found. Bon Appetit!

What to bring home from Genoa

Genoa is well-known for its mouthwatering cuisine, stunning architecture, and extensive cultural heritage. The following are some ideas for things you can take back from Genoa:

Pesto Genovese
Pesto was invented in Genoa, so you should bring home a few jars of the real thing. Look for pesto that is made with extra virgin olive oil, Parmesan cheese, garlic, Genovese basil, and pine nuts.

Focaccia

Genoa is also known for its delicious, soft, fluffy focaccia bread, which is topped with salt and olive oil. It is available at bakeries and from street vendors all over the city.

Pansoti

Pansoti is a customary Ligurian pasta loaded up with ricotta cheddar, spices, and greens. You can find dried pansoti in numerous food stores in Genoa, or you can take a stab at making your own without any preparation.

Products made by artisans

Genoa is home to a lot of talented artisans who make high-quality ceramics, leather goods, and textiles. Unique gifts and souvenirs can be found at local markets and boutiques.

Wines

Genoa has a lot of great local wines, and Liguria is a small but proud wine region. Vermentino-based white wines and Rossese di Dolceacqua-based red wines should be sought out.

Sweets

Canestrelli (crumbly cookies), pandolce (fruitcake), and amaretti (almond macaroons) are just a few of the delectable sweets and desserts that can be found in Genoa.

These are just a few suggestions for souvenirs you can take back to Genoa. Whatever you decide, don't forget to enjoy the flavors and memories of your trip to this wonderful city!

The Emilia-Romagna area of northern Italy is home to the lovely and historic city of Bologna. Travelers from all over the world flock to the city because of its beautiful architecture, extensive history, and delectable cuisine. The famous Two Towers, the Basilica di San Petronio, and the Fountain of Neptune are just a few of the magnificent structures that can be seen in Bologna's old center, which is among the best preserved in all of Europe. Bologna is an absolute must-see location that will leave you with priceless memories, whether you're interested in history, culture, cuisine, or simply want to soak up the ambiance of a stunning Italian city.

What to do in Bologna

In the northern part of Italy, Bologna is a stunning city with stunning architecture, delicious food, and a lively atmosphere. Here are a few things you can do in Bologna:

Go to the Piazza Maggiore

The center of Bologna and the city's main square are here. The Palazzo Comunale, the Basilica di San Petronio, and the renowned Fountain of Neptune are all within easy reach from here, making it an excellent starting point for your city tour.

Take the Asinelli Tower ascent

One of Italy's tallest leaning towers, this iconic structure provides breathtaking views of the city. To reach the top, you'll need to climb 498 steps!

Visit the Porticoes

Bologna is well known for its porticoes, which are covered walkways that line the roads. Over 38 kilometers of porticoes provide shade from the sun, rain, and snow in Bologna.

Try Bolognese food

Tortellini, lasagna, tagliatelle al ragù, and mortadella are just a few of the delectable dishes served in Bologna. Try these traditional dishes at one of the many restaurants in the area.

Visit the San Luca Asylum

The 3.8-kilometer portico that leads to this stunning church, which is perched on a hill with a view of the city below, can be walked up.

Visit Archiginnasio of Bologna

The Archiginnasio of Bologna is a historic structure Located in the city's core. One of the main attractions of the Archiginnasio is the Anatomical Theatre. Beautiful statues and frescoes adorn the walls of the room. The Ground Floor's Hall of Stabat Mater is another noteworthy aspect of the Archiginnasio. Previously used for graduation ceremonies, this hall is decorated with lovely frescoes.

Visit the Quadrilatero Industry

This vibrant and colorful market offers fresh produce, cheese, meat, fish, and other local goods for purchase. Experience the local culture and atmosphere in this wonderful location.

Check out the Two Towers

Another well-known symbol of Bologna is the Two Towers, also known as the Due Torri. They are a popular spot for taking photographs and are situated in the center of the city.

Bologna has a lot to offer, and these are just a few of them. Have a great trip!

Where to stay in Bologna

There are a lot of options for lodging in Bologna to suit different preferences and budgets. There are a few choices:

Hotels

There are many great hotels in Bologna, from budget to luxury. The majority of them are in the historic district, but there are numerous choices in other parts of the city.

Hotels and inns

In the historic center, Santo Stefano, and other residential areas, there are numerous bed and breakfasts. This option may be more affordable and provide a more individualized experience.

Apartments

If you are traveling with a group or intend to stay for a longer period, renting an apartment is a good option. A more authentic experience is provided by many apartments in the historic district.

Hostels

There are a few hostels in Bologna's historic center that provide backpackers and budget travelers with affordable lodging.

Agriturismo

Staying in an agritourism, a farm that caters to tourists, can provide you with a one-of-a-kind experience. In the countryside outside of Bologna, many agritourists provide a tranquil and authentic experience.

There are numerous lodging options in Bologna to choose from, regardless of your preference or budget. Be sure to make your reservations in advance, especially during peak travel times.

Where to eat in Bologna

The Emilia-Romagna region of Italy's capital, Bologna, is known for its extensive culinary history. Bologna's most well-liked eateries are as follows:

The Orsa Osteria

This cozy spot is well-known for its authentic Bolognese cuisine, which includes hearty meat dishes and handmade pasta.

Anna Maria Trattoria

Tortellini in brodo and tagliatelle al ragù are two of the homestyle dishes served at this restaurant, which is well-liked by the locals.

Gianni Restaurant

This rich café is a piece pricier, however worth the effort for the top-notch fixings and masterfully pre-arranged dishes. Try Tagliatelle with Bolognese sauce, a traditional Italian dish.

Tamburini Deli and Wine Bar

This shop and supermarket offer various new meats, cheeses, and other Italian delicacies, as well as an eating area where you can attempt their scrumptious sandwiches and panini.

Mezzo-Price Market
Prosciutto di Parma, Lambrusco wine, and Parmigiano Reggiano cheese are just a few of the local delicacies you can sample at this bustling food market.

The Il Guappo Pizza
A slice of delicious Neapolitan-style pizza, as well as other Italian favorites like lasagna and tiramisu, can be had at this casual establishment.

Gelateria Gianni
Polish off your feast with some genuine Italian gelato at this well-known spot, which offers different flavors made with new, occasional fixings.

Bologna has a lot of great restaurants, some of which are listed here. Whether you're searching for a comfortable trattoria or an extravagant café, you're certain to track down something heavenly in this foodie heaven.

What to bring home from Bologna

Beautiful Bologna has a rich culinary and cultural history. Some suggestions for what you can take back from Bologna are as follows:

Food and wine
Bologna is well known for its tasty food things as tortellini, tagliatelle, mortadella, Parmigiano Reggiano cheddar, and balsamic vinegar. These items are available at supermarkets, gourmet food shops, and local food markets. Lambrusco and Sangiovese are two of the finest wines produced in Bologna's Emilia-Romagna region. The wine shops in Bologna offer a wide selection of regional wines.

Craftmanship

Bologna is renowned for its conventional painstaking work, like ceramics, cowhide bags, belts, shoes, jackets, and hand-tailored paper. These are all available at local markets and shops.

Artisanal products
Numerous artisanal producers make one-of-a-kind goods like handmade soap, essential oils, and herbal remedies in Bologna. These goods are available at local markets and shops.

Fashion products
Bologna is a center point for Italian style, and you can find numerous neighborhood stores and shops selling planner garments, shoes, and embellishments.

Books
There are a lot of bookshops in Bologna that sell rare and one-of-a-kind books, and the city is also known for its long literary tradition.

Before bringing any food, wine, or handicrafts back to your home country, remember to check the customs rules there.

Italy's Tuscany area is home to the lovely cities of Pisa and Lucca. Both of them are renowned for their fascinating histories, magnificent buildings, and picturesque settings.

Most people know Pisa for its Leaning Tower, a bell tower that leans at an apparent angle because of its uneven base. For expansive views of the city and its surroundings, visitors can ascend to the tower's summit. The city is also home to other architectural gems including the Baptistery and the Pisa Cathedral, all of which feature stunning Romanesque design.

The walled city of Lucca is renowned for the preservation of its medieval core. Visitors can enjoy breathtaking views of the city and its surrounds from within the city's Renaissance-era walls, which are still standing today. Beautiful churches and palaces like the Palazzo Pfanner and the Cathedral of San Martino are also found in Lucca.

Pisa and Lucca are two wonderful urban communities in the Tuscany locale of Italy, both known for their verifiable and social attractions. Here are some thoughts on the best activities in Pisa and Lucca:

In Pisa:

Visit Pisa's Leaning Tower
One of the world's most well-known landmarks, the tower is Pisa's most popular attraction. You can get a great view of the city by climbing to the top.

Visit Piazza dei Miracoli
The Leaning Tower, the Cathedral of Pisa, the Baptistery, and the Camposanto Monumentale are all located on this square, which is also known as the Square of Miracles.

Visit the House of God of Pisa
The beautiful Romanesque-style cathedral known as the Cathedral of Santa Maria Assunta can be found in Piazza dei Miracoli. It has a lot of famous artworks in it, like the well-known pulpit by Giovanni Pisano.

Take a stroll by the Arno River
Take in the city's breathtaking views as you stroll along the riverbank. You can likewise lease a bicycle and cycle along the stream.

Take a tour of the city's heart
The charming historic center of Pisa is filled with numerous shops, cafes, and restaurants. Enjoy the vibrant atmosphere, the architecture, and the local street performers as you stroll around.

In Lucca:

Walk the city walls
Lucca's walls from the Renaissance era are well-known. On top of the walls, there is a four-kilometer path where you can bike or walk and get great views of the city.

Take a trip to Piazza dell'Anfiteatro
An ancient Roman amphitheater once stood on this singular oval-shaped square. It is now a bustling square with restaurants, cafes, and shops.

Visit the Guinigi Pinnacle
Move to the highest point of this pinnacle for breathtaking perspectives of the city and the encompassing slopes. The pinnacle is additionally popular for its roof garden with oak trees.

Visit the Church building of San Martino
The well-known tomb of Ilaria del Carretto, designed by Jacopo della Quercia, is one of many noteworthy works of art housed in this stunning Romanesque cathedral.

Take a trip to the Botanical Garden
The Orto Botanico di Lucca is a stunning garden that is home to a wide range of plants, some of which are rare and exotic. Relax and take in the natural beauty here.

Try some of the local food

Cecina, a savory chickpea pancake, and buccellato, a sweet bread with raisins, are two of Lucca's most famous dishes. Take advantage of this opportunity to try some of the local specialties!

Where to stay in Pisa & Lucca

There are many places to stay in Pisa, from cheap hostels to expensive hotels. A few famous regions to stay in Pisa include the notable downtown area, close to the Inclining Pinnacle, and close to the train station.

In Pisa:

The Bologna Hotel
This is situated close to the train station and offers beautiful rooms and an eatery serving conventional Tuscan food.

NH Pisa
The Leaning Tower can be reached on foot from this hotel, which has modern rooms and a rooftop terrace with city views.

Tower of Hostel Pisa
Dorms and private rooms are available at this affordable hostel, which is just a short walk from the Leaning Tower.

In Lucca:

Dipinto Palazzo
Elegant rooms with traditional decor are available at this guesthouse in the city center, which is housed in a historic building.

San Martino Hotel
This lodging is found right outside the city walls and offers beautiful rooms and a café serving conventional Tuscan food.

Hotel Villa La Principessa

This elegant hotel is located in the hills around Lucca and offers extensive rooms and a relaxing pool area.

Both Pisa and Lucca are delightful urban communities situated in Tuscany, Italy. They have a wide range of dining options to suit all tastes and budgets. The following are some suggestions for places to eat in Pisa and Lucca:

Pisa:

Osteria dei Cavalieri

This eatery is situated in the noteworthy focus of Pisa and serves conventional Tuscan dishes utilizing new, nearby fixings.

La Buca

La Buca is a cozy restaurant that serves tasty pasta and seafood at affordable prices.

Il Campano

Situated close to the Inclining Pinnacle of Pisa, Il Campano offers a delightful open-air seating region and serves incredible pizza, pasta, and meat dishes.

Lucca:

Trattoria Da Leo

This is a popular restaurant in the heart of Lucca that is renowned for its authentic Tuscan cuisine and welcoming atmosphere.

Buca di Sant'Antonio

This restaurant has been around since the 1700s and is a favorite with both locals and visitors. They offer a wide selection of wines and serve traditional Tuscan dishes.

Antica Drogheria
Antica Drogheria is a deli that has been converted into a restaurant. It serves homemade pasta dishes and delicious Italian meats and cheeses.

What to bring home from Pisa & Lucca

Both Pisa and Lucca are beautiful cities in Tuscany, Italy, and you can buy a variety of souvenirs and gifts there. Here are a few ideas:

Leather articles
Leather goods like wallets, belts, bags, and jackets can be found in both Pisa and Lucca. Tuscany is known for its leather goods.

Wine
Chianti and Brunello di Montalcino are two excellent wines from Tuscany that are also well-known. You can buy a few bottles of your favorite wine at a winery or shop in your area.

Olive oil
Some of Italy's best olive groves can be found in Tuscany, and Pisa and Lucca both produce high-quality extra virgin olive oil. Find small cans or bottles of olive oil produced locally to take home.

Pisan treats
"Torta coi bischeri," a dessert made with chestnut flour, and "biscotti di camaiore," almond biscuits, are two of Pisa's most well-known sweets available at local bakeries and pastry shops.

Souvenirs

You can also bring back postcards, magnets, and T-shirts with pictures of the leaning tower in Pisa or the old city walls in Lucca.

Before bringing back any wine or food products, remember to check customs regulations because some countries prohibit certain imports.

In the center of Tuscany stands the magnificent medieval city of Siena. Tourists frequently travel to the city because of its stunning architecture, extensive history, and vibrant culture. The Piazza del Campo, a sizable square regarded as one of the most beautiful in Italy, is among Siena's most well-known attractions. The Palio di Siena, a twice-yearly horse race, is held in the Piazza, which is surrounded by lovely structures. The Basilica of San Domenico, the Siena Cathedral, and other magnificent structures and landmarks are only a few examples of Siena's exquisite Gothic architecture. Additionally, visitors can explore the numerous stunning churches and museums that highlight Siena's extensive artistic and cultural heritage.

What to do in Siena

Siena is a lovely Italian city in the center of Tuscany. It is known for its breathtaking middle-age engineering, memorable milestones, and lovely open country. Siena offers the following activities:

Visit the Piazza del Campo
Siena's main square is also one of Italy's most well-known landmarks. It is a wonderful open space encompassed by noteworthy structures and the famous Fonte Gaia wellspring. Additionally, it is the location of the twice-yearly Palio horse race.

Visit the Siena Basilica
One of Italy's most impressive examples of Gothic architecture is this beautiful cathedral. It highlights breathtaking frescoes, multifaceted carvings, and a delightful marble exterior.

Visit the Public Palazzo

The famous frescoes of the Allegory of Good and Bad Government can be found here, which is the town hall of Siena. It has a beautiful courtyard, and a museum, and this is the building.

Explore the medieval streets
The old town of Siena is a maze of narrow streets and alleys lined with beautiful architecture and historic buildings. You can take in the atmosphere of this charming city and is the ideal location for walking exploration.

Go on a wine tour
Siena is in the center of Tuscany, one of the most well-known wine regions in Italy. In the surrounding countryside, there are numerous vineyards and wineries where you can sample some of Italy's finest wines and learn about winemaking.

Try some of the local food
Siena is known for its delicious food, which includes pasta, meat, cheeses, and wines made in the area. There are numerous eateries and bistros in the city where you can test the nearby cooking.

Visit the San Domenico Basilica
This wonderful church is home to the relics of Saint Catherine of Siena. It has lovely and exquisite pieces of art, including frescoes created by some of the most significant Sienese school artists, including Simone Martini and Ambrogio Lorenzetti. It has a tranquil cloister garden with lovely views of the surrounding hills that gives a pleasant escape from the bustle of the city.

Enjoy Torre del Mangia's view
This pinnacle is situated in Piazza del Campo and offers amazing views over the city and encompassing open country. The panoramic views are well worth the climb to the top of the stairs.

Take your time and see everything that Siena has to offer because there are so many more things to see and do.

There are numerous accommodation choices in Siena, Italy to suit various budgets and inclinations. The following are some possibilities:

Hotels
Hotels in Siena range from expensive to budget options. The Grand Hotel Continental, the Hotel Athena, and the Hotel Palazzo di Valli are a few of Siena's most well-known luxury hotels. Hotel Moderno, Hotel Porta Romana, and Hotel Minerva are good choices for those on a budget.

B&Bs
Siena's hospitality and culture can be experienced at bed and breakfasts. Some famous B&Bs in Siena are B&B La Coperta Ricamata, B&B Le Logge del Father, and B&B Il Corso.

Apartments
Renting an apartment in Siena can be a good option if you are traveling with friends or family. Numerous apartments can be found on well-known booking platforms like Airbnb, Booking.com, and HomeAway.

Hostels
There are a few hostels in Siena, which can be a good option for travelers on a budget. Inn Siena is a well-known inn in the city.

Consider factors like location, amenities, and reviews from previous guests when selecting a lodging option. Because Siena is such a popular tourist destination, it is best to reserve your lodging in advance to avoid disappointment.

Siena is a delightful city in Tuscany, Italy, known for its staggering middle-aged engineering, exhibition halls, and lovely open country. Siena has a lot of great restaurants that serve both contemporary Italian fare and traditional Tuscan fare. The following are some suggestions:

Osteria Le Logge
This is a well-known restaurant in the historic city center that serves authentic Tuscan dishes like pappardelle with wild boar sauce, Chianina beef, and truffles, among others. Additionally, the restaurant offers a comprehensive wine list that includes both regional and local wines.

Trattoria La Torre
In the heart of Siena, Trattoria La Torre is another excellent restaurant. It serves delicious homemade pasta dishes like pici with meat sauce and gnocchi with gorgonzola cheese sauce. In addition, the restaurant has a great selection of vegetarian dishes, seafood, and grilled meats.

Ristorante Guidoriccio
This is a charming restaurant with great views of the countryside that can be found just outside the city walls. Steak, seafood, and homemade pasta are just a few of the modern twists of traditional Tuscan cuisine on the menu.

Il Canto del Maggio
Il Canto del Maggio has stunning views of the surrounding countryside and is in the hills just outside of Siena. Homemade pasta, grilled meats, and vegetarian options are among the inventive Tuscan dishes on the menu, which make use of seasonal,

fresh ingredients. Additionally, the restaurant offers a comprehensive wine list that includes both regional and local wines.

Enoteca I Terzi
A wine bar and café situated in the core of Siena's notable community, Enoteca I Terzi is an extraordinary spot to take a glass of wine and a couple of little plates. Traditional Tuscan dishes like crostini with chicken liver pate, grilled vegetables, and cured meats are on the menu.

These are only a couple of the numerous extraordinary spots to eat in Siena. You can likewise Visit the city's numerous bistros, gelaterias, and bread shops to attempt nearby fortes like panforte (a customary Tuscan cake) and gelato.

What to bring home from Siena

Siena, situated in the core of Tuscany, Italy, is a city wealthy ever, craftsmanship, and culture. You could bring home some souvenirs from Siena like these:

Panforte
Honey, nuts, and candied fruit go into this popular Sienese dessert, which is a popular souvenir.

Wine
Siena is no exception to Tuscany's reputation for producing excellent wines. You could bring back a jug of Chianti, Brunello di Montalcino, or Vino Nobile di Montepulciano, which are all created in the locale.

Pecorino cheese
This cheese made with sheep's milk is a local specialty in Siena and can be found in a lot of shops all over the city.

Ceramic artifacts
Handmade pottery in a wide range of styles and colors is a hallmark of Siena. Look for pieces with traditional Tuscan designs like grapevines or sunflowers.

Leather articles
Italy is popular for its cowhide, and Siena is no special case. You could bring back a calfskin sack, wallet, or belt as a trinket.

Handicrafts
Numerous artisans who make handcrafted goods like jewelry, textiles, and wood carvings reside in Siena. Find things that are influenced by the culture and history of the city.

Saffron
Siena is one of only a handful of exceptional spots in Italy where saffron is delivered. You could bring a small container of this prized spice, which is used in a lot of Italian dishes, back with you.

In general, Siena offers different keepsakes that mirror its rich social legacy and neighborhood fortes.

CHAPTER 10: ASSISI

The little town of Assisi is situated in central Italy's Umbria region. The Catholic saint St. Francis of Assisi, who established the Franciscan order, was born in the town, earning it fame as his birthplace. The Basilica di San Francesco, a massive church complex devoted to St. Francis, is one of Assisi's most well-known attractions. There are numerous other stunning churches and structures in Assisi, including the Basilica di Santa Maria degli Angeli. Assisi is particularly well-known for its delectable food, which uses a variety of regional specialties from Umbria, including lentils, wild boar, and truffles. Additionally, tourists can savor regional wines like the Sagrantino di Montefalco.

What to do in Assisi

Assisi is a lovely peak town in Umbria, Italy, known for its middle-age engineering, strict importance, and breathtaking perspectives on the Umbrian open country. In Assisi, you can do the following:

The Basilica of Saint Francis of Assisi
This impressive church is a UNESCO World Heritage Site and is dedicated to Saint Francis, the patron saint of Italy. Numerous stunning frescoes by well-known Italian artists, including Giotto, can be found inside the basilica.

Take in the historic district
You'll feel like you've stepped back in time as you stroll through the historic center of Assisi's narrow streets. In addition to charming shops and restaurants, you'll find numerous medieval structures like churches and palaces.

Walk the walls

The ancient walls that surround Assisi provide breathtaking views of the surrounding valleys and hills. Take in the scenery as you stroll along the walls.

Visit the San Rufino Cathedral
This Romanesque cathedral is one of the most established places of worship in Assisi and is dedicated to Saint Rufinus, the first bishop of Assisi. Numerous significant pieces of art are housed in the cathedral, including Cimabue frescoes. The tomb of Saint Rufinus and the baptismal font where Saint Francis of Assisi was baptized are only two of the significant relics and artifacts that can be found inside the cathedral.

Visit the Santa Chiara Basilica
The stunning rose window and frescoes of this basilica, which is named after Saint Clare, one of Saint Francis' followers, are well-known.

Take a cooking class
Assisi is known for its tasty cooking, so why not figure out how to make a portion of the neighborhood strengths? Classes at many cooking schools teach you how to make pizza, pasta, and other Italian dishes.

Take a tour of wineries
Since Umbria is well-known for its excellent wines, why not take a tour of some of the region's wineries and try some of the region's most recent releases?

Participate in a festival
Numerous festivals take place throughout the year in Assisi, one of which is the Calendimaggio in May, which marks the beginning of spring. Assisi's streets and buildings are festooned with flags, banners, and flowers. The event, which features music, dance, and

pageantry, is marked by rivalry between the city's "Parte de Sopra" and "Parte de Sotto" districts.

These are only a couple of what should be done in Assisi. This charming Italian town is sure to have something to offer you no matter what you like to do.

Where to stay in Assisi

There are a variety of lodging choices in Assisi to suit a variety of budgets and preferences. The following are a couple of ideas for where to stay in Assisi:

The Subasio Hotel In the heart of Assisi
This charming hotel has stunning views of the Umbrian countryside. The staff is friendly and helpful, and the rooms are large and comfortable.

The Nun Assisi Relais and Spa
Beautiful frescoes and other works of art decorate this opulent hotel, which is housed in a former convent. The rooms are exquisite and roomy, and the spa offers a scope of medicines to help you unwind and loosen up.

Palace Hotel Fontebella Assisi
This exquisite lodging is situated in a memorable structure and offers lovely perspectives on the valley. The restaurant serves delectable Umbrian cuisine, and the rooms are large and well-appointed.

Pax Hotels
The historic center of Assisi is just a short walk away from this affordable hotel. The staff is friendly and helpful, and the rooms are basic but comfortable.

Poggio degli Olivi Agritourism
Consider staying at this charming agriturismo just outside of Assisi for a more rural experience. The property has stunning views of the countryside, and the rooms are large and comfortable.

Where to eat in Assisi

In the Umbria region of Italy, Assisi is a beautiful town known for its stunning views and religious history. The following are some recommended eateries in Assisi:

Osteria Piazzetta dell'erba
Traditional Umbrian fare, including delectable truffles and other regional specialties, can be found at this restaurant. It has a comfortable climate and is situated in the core of the old town.

Pallotta Trattoria
This café offers a blend of exemplary Italian and nearby Umbrian cooking, including high-quality pasta dishes and simmered meats. There is a lovely terrace with views of the countryside.

Metastasio's Restaurant
A refined menu of Italian and international dishes can be found at this elegant restaurant, which is housed in a historic building. It has a wonderful open-air patio and a wine basement loaded with brilliant neighborhood and global wines.

Cesare's Eatery
The homemade pasta and grilled meats that this rustic trattoria serves are famous for are among the best in the region. It is in the heart of the historic district and has a warm atmosphere.

Taverna dei Consoli

There are truffles, wild boar, and roasted meats on the traditional Umbrian menu at this restaurant. It is in a lovely spot with a view of the town's main square.

In Assisi, there are numerous dining options. You can be sure to enjoy delicious local cuisine and beautiful surroundings wherever you dine.

What to bring home from Assisi

Assisi, situated in focal Italy, is a city of verifiable and social importance, and there are a few special things you can think about bringing back as trinkets. The following are a couple of ideas:

Religious items
Since St. Francis, Italy's patron saint, was born in Assisi, you won't be surprised to find many religious items there. Medals, statues, rosaries, and crosses are examples of these.

Olive oil
Olive groves cover the hills surrounding Assisi, and the region produces some of Italy's finest olive oil. Find extra-virgin olive oil bottles made locally to take home.

Porcelain
Hand-painted porcelain is renowned in the nearby town of Deruta. Plates, bowls, and other pieces of tableware can be found with intricate designs.

Cowhide merchandise
Assisi is no exception to Italy's reputation for producing goods made of high-quality leather. Italian leather jackets, wallets, belts, and handbags should be on your lookout.

Wine

Sagrantino di Montefalco and Torgiano Rosso Riserva are two excellent wines from Umbria, where Assisi is located. Bottles can be found at nearby wine shops.

Truffles
Umbria is additionally known for its truffles, particularly dark truffles. To take home, look for truffle oil or paste jars.

High-quality crafts
Assisi has a rich practice of high-quality things, including stoneware, woven materials, and wooden items. Unique keepsakes can be found in handcrafted shops.

CHAPTER 11: NAPLES

Naples, a dynamic city in southern Italy's Campania region, is renowned for its fascinating history, beautiful architecture, and delectable cuisine. The city is located on the Bay of Naples with the beautiful Mount Vesuvius looming in the distance. The historic city center of Naples, which is home to numerous stunning structures and landmarks like the Naples Cathedral, the Castel dell'Ovo, and the Royal Palace of Naples, is one of the city's most well-liked attractions. Visitors can also wander around the numerous, winding streets and alleyways that are dotted with boutiques, cafes, and eateries.

What to do in Naples

Naples is a stunning city in southern Italy that is renowned for its exquisite cuisine, stunning architecture, and rich history. In Naples, you can do the following:

Go to Pompeii
In 79 AD, Mount Vesuvius erupted, destroying the ancient Roman city of Pompeii. From Naples, you can take a day trip to see the ruins and learn about ancient life.

Visit the historic district
This is a UNESCO World Heritage Site that provides tourists with a window into the city's past. The numerous churches, some of which are from the Middle Ages, are one of the district's main draws. The historic district is also home to some palaces that provide a window into the affluent and powerful people's lifestyles during the Renaissance and Baroque periods. Visiting one of the many museums that highlight the city's rich cultural heritage would round out any trip to the historic district. One of the most spectacular is the Museo Archeologico Nazionale, which houses a sizable collection of antiquities such as sculptures, mosaics, and even the infamous "Secret Cabinet" that houses erotic art from Pompeii.

Eat pizza
Since pizza was invented in Naples, you must try the traditional Neapolitan pizza there. Probably the best pizza places in Naples include Pizza joint Da Michele and Pizza joint Sorbillo.

National Archaeological Museum
Mosaics, frescoes, and sculptures from Pompeii and Herculaneum can be found in this museum's extensive collection.

Take a stroll along the coast
Naples has a delightful seafront promenade called Lungomare that is ideally suited for a relaxed walk. The stunning views of Mount Vesuvius and the Bay of Naples are available to you.

Visit the Castle of Ovo
This middle age palace is situated on a little island in the Straight of Naples and is one of the city's most notorious milestones.

Attempt the neighborhood cooking

Naples is known for its delicious seafood dishes, pasta, and pastries, as well as pizza. Sfogliatelle, a shell-shaped pastry filled with ricotta cheese, and spaghetti alle vongole, also known as spaghetti with clams, should be on your menu.

Visit the Mausoleums of San Gennaro

These sepulchers are an underground graveyard that traces back to the early Christian time. They are a one-of-a-kind and fascinating place to visit, and they are in the suburbs of Naples.

Go to Capri on a great day trip

Capri is a delightful island situated off the bank of Naples and is well known for its breathtaking landscape and completely clear waters. You can spend the day exploring Capri by taking a ferry from Naples.

Where to stay in Naples

If you're searching for accommodation in Naples, there are various choices accessible relying on your budget and inclinations. Some suggestions are as follows:

Hotels
There are numerous hotels in Naples, ranging from budget-friendly options to luxurious establishments. The Grand Hotel Vesuvio, Hotel Royal Continental, and the Hotel San Francesco Al Monte are a few of the most well-liked alternatives.

B&Bs
There are a lot of bed and breakfasts in Naples if you want a more personal and intimate experience. The B&B Villa San Gennariello and the B&B La Dimora di Nettuno are two of the most well-known ones.

Airbnb
Naples has an enormous number of Airbnb postings, from private rooms to whole condos or houses. If you're looking for more space and flexibility, this might be a good choice.

Hostels
Several hostels in Naples provide affordable lodging for travelers on a tight budget. The Hostel of the Sun and the La Controra Hostel Naples are two well-liked choices.

Notwithstanding which choice you pick, it's generally really smart to understand surveys and do your exploration ahead of time to guarantee that you're getting the most ideal experience.

Where to eat in Naples

Naples is renowned for its tasty and valid Italian cooking. Here are a portion of the top spots to eat in Naples:

Michele's Pizzeria
This well-known pizzeria has been around since 1870 and is famous for its Margherita pizza, which is simple but delicious.

Sorbillo
Another well-known pizzeria, Sorbillo serves fresh, high-quality Neapolitan pizzas in a wide variety of flavors.

Trattoria da Nennella
Classic Neapolitan fare like pasta with fresh seafood and meatballs in tomato sauce can be found at this charming trattoria.

The Gusto Stanza
The contemporary interpretation of traditional Neapolitan cuisine offered by this posh restaurant emphasizes making use of products sourced from nearby sources.

Il Contra
This road food stand is popular for its broiled fish, served in a cone.

Pizzeria Antica Port'Alba
Antica Pizzeria Port'Alba serves delicious Neapolitan pizzas with a crispy crust and fresh toppings, claiming to be the world's oldest pizzeria.

The Buonumore Oven
A comfortable eatery with an extraordinary climate, Osteria del Buonumore offers a menu of customary Neapolitan dishes and magnificent wine choices.

The Old Pizzeria Michele
This is one more area of the well-known Pizza joint da Michele, so you can enjoy a similar scrumptious pizza in an alternate area of the city.

Naples has a lot of great restaurants, some of which are listed here. In this lively city, you're sure to find something delicious, whether you're looking for contemporary Italian fare or traditional Neapolitan fare.

What to bring home from Naples

Naples is a city in southern Italy known for its rich history, culture, and cooking. Here are some suggestions for things to bring back from Naples as mementos or gifts:

Neapolitan espresso
Coffee from Neapolitan is well-known for its robust flavor. You can bring home a bag of coffee beans or pre-ground coffee.

Limoncello
Limoncello is a popular sweet-and-sour lemon liqueur in Naples. In Naples, limoncello can be purchased in numerous supermarkets and shops.

Ceramics
Ceramics in Naples are renowned for their beauty and vibrant colors. Intricate patterns and designs can be found on a wide range of ceramics, including plates, cups, and vases.

Pizza
Since Naples is known as the birthplace of pizza, it should come as no surprise that the city produces some of the world's finest pizza. Consider bringing back a pizza-making kit or pizza-related souvenirs if you enjoy pizza.

Cameos
Cameos, which are small carved stones or shells that are used to make jewelry and other decorative items, are a specialty of Naples. In Naples, cameos can be found in numerous shops and markets.

Taralli

Taralli is little, crunchy breadsticks that are well known in Naples and different pieces of southern Italy. They come in a variety of flavors, including black pepper, fennel, and garlic.

Sfogliatella

Sfogliatella is a customary Neapolitan cake that is made with layers of slight, flaky baked goods and loaded up with sweet ricotta cheddar. You can track down these heavenly cakes in numerous pastry kitchens and bistros in Naples.

Souvenirs and t-shirts

The colors and symbols of Naples can be seen on a wide range of souvenirs, including t-shirts, keychains, magnets, and other items. These make excellent presents for domestic friends and family.

CHAPTER 12: POMPEII

Pompeii is an ancient Roman city that was ruined and buried by Mount Vesuvius' eruption in 79 AD. Pompeii is now one of Italy's most famous tourist destinations. The city was unearthed in the 18th century, and excavations have continued ever since, giving an intriguing peek into ancient Roman life. Visitors can walk through the streets and structures of the city, which have been preserved by volcanic ash and offer a unique view of daily life in Roman times. The Forum, a vast public space where political and social events would take place, and the House of the Vettii, a well-preserved aristocratic mansion that shows the exquisite mosaics and frescoes that were popular, are two of Pompeii's most popular attractions.

What to do in Pompeii

One of Italy's most popular archaeological sites is Pompeii, which is listed on the UNESCO World Heritage List. The following are some things to do in Pompeii and the surrounding area:

Visit the Pompeii Archeological Site
The ruins of the ancient Roman city that were destroyed by the eruption of Mount Vesuvius in 79 AD can be seen here, which is the main attraction in Pompeii. You could spend an entire day exploring the vast site.

Visit the city of Naples
Naples is Italy's third-largest city, renowned for its fascinating past, stunning architecture, and mouthwatering cuisine. The Naples National Archaeological Museum, the Royal Palace of Naples, and the Castel dell'Ovo are all worth a visit.

Mount Vesuvius ascent

Mount Vesuvius is the spring of gushing lava that emitted and obliterated Pompeii. It is possible to ascend to the summit and take in breathtaking views of the landscape that surrounds you. Guided tours are available.

Check out Herculaneum
Herculaneum is one more Roman city that was annihilated by the ejection of Mount Vesuvius. Although it is smaller than Pompeii, the ruins are better preserved and there are fewer people there.

Capri day trip
Capri is a popular tourist destination that is a small island off the coast of Naples. You can take a ship from Naples and go through a day investigating the island, visiting the Blue Cavern, and enjoying the seashores.

You can go to the Amalfi Coast
The Amalfi Coast, south of Naples, is a stunning stretch of coastline known for its picturesque towns, breathtaking views, and delectable cuisine. Take a drive along the coast, check out the towns of Amalfi, Positano, and Ravello, and try some of the food from those areas.

Check the remnants of Paestum
South of Naples is the ancient Greek city of Paestum. It is known for its all-around saved sanctuaries and antiquated ruins, including the Sanctuary of Hera and the Sanctuary of Athena. If you are interested in ancient history, this is a fantastic location to explore.

Visit the Illustrious Royal residence of Caserta
The Bourbon Kings of Naples used to live in the Royal Palace of Caserta, which is a UNESCO World Heritage Site. It is one of Italy's most impressive palaces and is known for its stunning architecture, gardens, and fountains.

Capua's Roman Amphitheater

The ancient Roman city of Capua was located north of Naples. It is well-known for its Roman amphitheater, which can hold up to 30,000 people. It is an extraordinary spot to visit if you are keen on Roman history.

Take a cooking class

Taking a cooking class is a great way to learn about the food culture in Naples, which is known for its delicious cuisine. Local chefs can teach you how to make pizza, pasta, and other Italian dishes.

Generally speaking, there is no lack of activities in Pompeii and the close by regions. This region of Italy has something for everyone, whether you're interested in ancient history, stunning architecture, delicious food, or stunning scenery.

Where to stay in Pompeii

In Pompei, you can choose from a wide range of lodging options to fit your needs and budget. A few suggestions are as follows:

Hotel Forum

This is an exceptionally ranked lodging found right close to the old vestiges of Pompeii. It has air-conditioned, comfortable rooms, a rooftop terrace, and a restaurant that serves traditional Italian food.

The La Medusa Hotel and Spa

In a peaceful part of Castellammare di Stabia, this luxurious hotel is just a short drive from Pompeii. It has a spa, a pool, a lovely garden, and rooms that are spacious and elegant.

Hotel Amleto

This is an affordable hotel that is only a stone-throw away from the Pompeii archeological site. It has a restaurant that serves regional fare and has basic rooms with air conditioning.

Agriturismo Vivinatura Hotel Country Resort
This is a beguiling farmhouse situated in the field close to Pompeii. It has rooms with rustic decor and a restaurant where local ingredients are used to make homemade food.

Hotel Santa Caterina
The archaeological site is just a short walk away from this historic hotel in the heart of Pompeii. The rooftop terrace has a view of Mount Vesuvius and elegant rooms with antique furniture.

Villa Franca
A restored 19th-century villa in the town of Boscoreale, just a few kilometers from Pompeii, houses this boutique hotel. It has a garden, rooms that are stylish and spacious and a restaurant that serves traditional cuisine.

Hotel Pompeii
A contemporary hotel can be found just a short distance away from the Pompeii archeological site. It offers beautiful rooms with cooling and a housetop porch with perspectives on the encompassing region.

Pompei Resort
This is a substantial hotel just outside of Pompeii. It provides standard rooms as well as suites with hot tubs in a variety of configurations. Additionally, it has a restaurant that serves Italian and international cuisine, a spa, and a pool.

Bed & Breakfast La Casa di Plinio
Bed and Breakfast The archaeological site is just a short walk from this bed and breakfast in the heart of Pompeii. It has air-conditioned, comfortable rooms, a shared kitchen, and a terrace.

There are a lot of places to eat in Pompeii, from pizzerias and casual cafes to fancy restaurants that serve traditional Neapolitan food. The following are some suggestions for places to eat in Pompeii:

La Bettola del Gusto
Just outside the archaeological site's entrance is this popular restaurant. In addition to a wide selection of wines, it serves up traditional Neapolitan fare, such as pizza, seafood, and pasta.

Pizzeria La Primavera
This is a family-run pizza joint situated in the focal point of Pompeii. It offers flavorful wood-terminated pizza, as well as other exemplary Italian dishes.

Bacco Ristorante
In the heart of Pompeii, in a historic building, you'll find this elegant restaurant. It uses fresh, local ingredients to creatively reimagine traditional Neapolitan cuisine.

Osteria dei Principi
This cozy restaurant is just outside of Pompeii's center. It serves seafood, pasta, and meat dishes from the traditional Italian menu.

Il Principe
This is a la mode eatery situated in the close by town of Castellammare di Stabia, around 10 kilometers from Pompeii. It offers a menu of contemporary Italian cooking, as well as a broad wine list.

What to bring home from Pompeii

Ancient Roman life can be seen at Pompeii, a fascinating archaeological site. Even though you are unable to bring any artifacts back from the site, you can still purchase numerous mementos and souvenirs to remember your visit. Some ideas are as follows:

Souvenirs about Pompeii
In the gift shops around the site, you can find a variety of Pompeii-themed souvenirs like postcards, magnets, keychains, and t-shirts.

Nearby food and drink
The wine, olive oil, limoncello, and other local delicacies of Campania, where Pompeii is located, are well-known. These items can be found in local specialty shops.

Craftsman-made goods
The handmade ceramics that are made in the nearby town of Sorrento are well-known, and you can find beautiful pieces in the shops around Pompeii.

Guidebooks and books
There are a lot of books and guides available in the gift shops and bookstores around the site if you want to learn more about Pompeii and its history.

Photographs and recollections
Last but not least, don't forget to snap a lot of pictures and create memories that will last a lifetime!

The Amalfi Coast and Paestum are two of southern Italy's most renowned tourist sites, recognized for their beautiful beauty, rich history, and vibrant culture.

The Amalfi Coast is a stretch of coastline in southern Italy's Campania region famed for its scenic villages, craggy cliffs, and crystal-clear waters. Positano, Amalfi, and Ravello are three of the most popular towns along the coast, each with its distinct charm and attractions.

Paestum, on the other hand, is an ancient Greek city near the Amalfi Coast in the province of Salerno. The city was founded in the sixth century BC and served as a significant commerce and cultural center during the Greek and Roman periods.

What to do in Amalfi Coast and Paestum

Paestum and the Amalfi Coast are two stunning locations in Italy's Campania region that provide a wide range of activities and sights for tourists. In each location, there are some things to do:

Amalfi Coast:

Enjoy the scenic drive
The stunning views and winding roads of the Amalfi Coast are what makes it so famous. Take a bus tour or rent a car to see the stunning coastline and charming villages.

To go to Positano
The colorful buildings and steep streets of this charming village are well-known. Explore the beaches, cafes, and shops for a day.

Take a Deity's Footsteps
This fabulous climbing trail offers unimaginable perspectives on the shore and takes you through little towns and past old vestiges.

Take a tour by boat
Take a boat tour to see the Amalfi Coast from the water. You can visit secluded coves and beaches and get a unique look at the coastline.

Go to Ravello
The stunning views and beautiful gardens of this hilltop town are well-known. The gardens of Villa Cimbrone and Villa Rufolo should not be missed.

Paestum:

Take a look at the ancient ruins
Paestum is home to the absolute best-protected antiquated Greek sanctuaries on the planet. Spend the day touring the museum, amphitheater, and temples.

Try the buffalo mozzarella
Paestum's buffalo mozzarella, which is made from the milk of water buffalo, is also well-known. You can see how this delicious cheese is made and sample some by going to a nearby farm.

Go on a beach trip
The long sandy beach in Paestum is ideal for swimming and sunbathing.

Take a tour by bike
Lease a bicycle and Visit the wide open around Paestum. Vineyards, olive groves, and small villages will be visible to you.

Participate in a festival
Throughout the year, Paestum plays host to a Buffalo Festival and a Greek Festival. Take a look at the timetable to check whether any occasions are occurring during your visit.

Where to stay in Amalfi Coast and Paestum

Depending on your preferences and budget, Paestum and the Amalfi Coast offer a wide range of lodging options. There are a few choices:

Amalfi Coast:

Luxurious Inns
The luxurious hotels on the Amalfi Coast are well known for their breathtaking views. The Belmond Hotel Caruso, the Hotel Santa Caterina, and the Palazzo Avino are among the best choices.

Boutique hotels

Consider staying at a boutique hotel like the Casa Angelina or the Monastero Santa Rosa Hotel & Spa for a more intimate and unique experience.

B&Bs
You can stay at a bed and breakfast like the La Casa degli Dei or the Villa Maria Luigia for a more local experience.

Rental Apartments
The Amalfi Coast has a lot of options for vacation rentals, from apartments to villas with private pools. Airbnb and VRBO are two well-known places to look for these rentals.

Paestum:

Agriturismo
Agriturismo, or farmhouses that provide lodging and meals, are a popular choice for visitors to Paestum, which is in a rural region of southern Italy. The Agriturismo La Vecchia Quercia and the Agriturismo Seliano are two options in Paestum.

Hotels
In Paestum, there are also hotels like the Savoy Beach Hotel and the Hotel dei Templi.

B&Bs
You can likewise track down overnight B&B choices in Paestum, for example, the B&B Casa Rubini and the B&B Il Granaio dei Casabella.

Rental Apartments
Lastly, Paestum offers a variety of vacation rental options, including villas and apartments. These rentals can be found on websites like Airbnb and HomeAway.

The Amalfi Coast and Paestum are well known for their delectable food, including new fish, high-quality pasta, and privately developed produce. The following are some suggested eateries in each location:

Amalfi Coast:

Positanian Sponda
The Le Sirenuse Hotel in Positano has a Michelin-starred restaurant that provides an unforgettable dining experience.

Il Flauto di Container (Amalfi)
This restaurant serves delicious seafood and pasta dishes in a beautiful historic building in the heart of Amalfi.

Trattoria Cumpa Cosimo (Ravello)
For more than 60 years, this family-owned restaurant has been serving traditional Amalfi Coast cuisine. It is well-known for its mouthwatering pasta dishes and fresh seafood.

Paestum:

Il Granaio dei Casabella
This farm-to-table restaurant serves delectable seasonal dishes made with products grown in the area. It is just a short drive from the Paestum archaeological site.

Paestum's Osteria del Mare
This seafood restaurant, which is in the center of Paestum, serves a wide range of fresh seafood dishes, including their renowned clam spaghetti.

Hotel Ristorante La Selva

This comfortable café is situated on the slopes above Paestum and offers flavorful hand-crafted pasta dishes and nearby fortes, including bison mozzarella and barbecued meats.

In general, both the Amalfi Coast and Paestum have a lot of great restaurants, from fine dining establishments to more casual trattorias and osterias. Make it a point to try some of the regional specialties and take in the clean flavors of Mediterranean cuisine.

What to bring home from Amalfi Coast and Paestum

Paestum and the Amalfi Coast have a lot to offer in terms of souvenirs and local specialties. Some suggestions are as follows:

Limoncello
A well-liked memento, this sweet lemon liqueur is made from the region's lemons. The majority of shops and markets along the Amalfi Coast sell bottles of limoncello.

Ceramics
The colorful and intricate ceramics of the Amalfi Coast are well known for their beauty as gifts and decorative items. You can track down pottery at shops and markets all through the area.

Positano design
Positano's fashion is well-known, especially for its beachwear and brightly colored linen clothing. All over the town, there are shops and boutiques where you can find clothing and accessories.

Buffalo mozzarella
Paestum is situated in the core of the bison mozzarella locale, and you can track down this scrumptious cheddar at business sectors and shops all through the town.

Olive oil

The area around Paestum is known for its top-notch olive oil, produced using the nearby olives. Olive oil can be purchased in bottles at local markets and shops.

Souvenirs from Ancient Greece
The Paestum archaeological site has some of Italy's best-preserved ancient Greek temples, and the site's gift shop has replicas and souvenirs of ancient Greek artifacts.

Overall, the Amalfi Coast and Paestum have a lot of great souvenirs and specialties that show off the unique culture, cuisine, and history of these beautiful places.

CHAPTER 14: SORRENTO & CAPRI

Sorrento and Capri are two lovely destinations in southern Italy's Campania region, recognized for their stunning natural beauty, rich history, and vibrant culture.

Sorrento is a lovely village on the Sorrentine Peninsula with views of the Bay of Naples. It is famous for its magnificent beaches, winding lanes, and breathtaking views of Mount Vesuvius. Visitors can stroll along the promenade overlooking the sea or explore the town's historic core, which is lined with colorful buildings and stores selling local products.

Capri is a lovely island in the Bay of Naples famed for its magnificent beaches, clean waters, and cliffs. Visitors can take a boat excursion around the island to discover hidden coves and grottos, or they can explore the picturesque towns and villages.

Sorrento and Capri are must-see places that will leave you with wonderful memories, whether you're interested in natural beauty, and history, or simply want to enjoy the charm of little Italian villages.

Sorrento and Capri are both delightful objections in Italy that offer different exercises for guests. In Sorrento and Capri, you can do the following:

Sorrento:

Take a tour of the old town
Sorrento's old town is brimming with enchanting roads, memorable structures, and conventional shops and eateries. Take a stroll to learn about the culture.

Go to the beach
The stunning beaches of Sorrento are well-known. Probably the most well-known ones are Marina Grande, Marina Piccola, and the Showers of Sovereign Giovanna.

Take a cooking class
Since Sorrento is known for its delicious food, why not learn how to prepare some of the local specialties? Classes for tourists are offered by several cooking schools.

Check out the museums
The Correale Museum of Terranova and the Museo Bottega della Tarsia Lignea are two of Sorrento's museums that highlight the art and history of the city.

Go for a day trip

From Sorrento, you can easily visit Pompeii, Naples, the Amalfi Coast, and other nearby destinations.

Capri:

Take a tour by boat:
The sea is one of the best ways to see the island of Capri. The Blue Grotto and the coastline can be seen from the water on boat tours.

The Blue Grotto
The bright blue water of the Blue Grotto, a sea cave, is well-known. Guests can bring a little boat into the cavern to encounter its magnificence very close.

Visit the town of Capri
High-end stores, restaurants, and historic structures like the Villa San Michele and the Gardens of Augustus abound in Capri.

Take a hike to Monte Solaro's peak
The island's highest point, Monte Solaro, provides stunning views of the surrounding landscape. The summit can be reached by foot or via chairlift.

Visit the Faraglioni rock arrangements
One of Capri's most well-known landmarks is the trio of towering rock formations known as the Faraglioni. For a closer look, visitors can hike or take a boat tour.

Where to stay in Sorrento & Capri

There are many places to stay in Italy's popular tourist destinations of Sorrento and Capri. Some suggestions are as follows:

Sorrento:

The Grand Hotel Excelsior Vittoria

This is a five-star luxury hotel in the center of Sorrento. It has stunning views of the sea.

Hotel Bellevue Syrene

Another 5-star hotel with a romantic atmosphere and a rooftop terrace with views of the Bay of Naples is the Bellevue Syrene.

Comfort Hotel Gardenia

The charming boutique Comfort Hotel Gardenia is just a short walk from Sorrento's center and features a pool, a beautiful garden, and other amenities.

Maison La Minervetta

This is a polished lodging with an extraordinary plan and stunning perspectives on the ocean.

Capri:

Anacapri's Capri Palace

This is a five-star resort with a pool, spa, and Michelin-starred restaurant.

The J.K. Place Capri

This is a boutique hotel in the center of Capri with a gorgeous garden and chic decor inspired by the Mediterranean.

Hotel La Scalinatella

In a quiet area of Capri, the charming hotel La Scalinatella has a lovely terrace with a view of the sea and a peaceful atmosphere.

Hotel Punta Tragara

The 5-star Hotel Punta Tragara is on a stunning cliffside with stunning views of the sea and the Faraglioni rocks.

Italy's beautiful islands of Capri and Sorrento offer a wide range of delicious dining options. The following are some recommendations for restaurants in Sorrento and Capri:

Sorrento:

Ristorante Bagni Delfino
This is a great seafood restaurant with stunning views of the Mediterranean Sea in a great location. Fresh seafood and traditional Italian dishes abound on the menu.

Il Buco
This eatery has a comfortable and heartfelt climate and is known for its custom-made pasta, fish, and meat dishes.

Zi'Ntonio
This is a family-run café that serves credible Neapolitan cooking, including pizza, fish, and pasta. Additionally, the restaurant has an excellent wine selection.

La Cantinaccia del Popolo
This is a restaurant in Sorrento's historic center that serves a contemporary take on traditional dishes. There are seafood, meat, and vegetarian options available on the menu.

Capri:

Aurora
This Michelin-featured café is situated in the core of Capri and offers an imaginative menu of Mediterranean and Neapolitan cooking. Additionally, the restaurant has a magnificent wine cellar.

Da Paolino

This eatery is renowned for its lemon trees, which make a lovely climate. The menu highlights conventional Caprese cooking, including fish, pasta, and meat dishes.

La Fontelina
This café is situated on the rocks sitting above the ocean, and it is a famous spot for lunch. The views are breathtaking, and the menu includes pasta, salads, and seafood dishes.

Ristorante Michelangelo
This is well-known for its expansive sea and island views. The menu includes seafood, meat, and pasta dishes typical of Caprese cuisine.

What to bring home in Sorrento & Capri

Sorrento and Capri are both popular for their one-of-a-kind and great items. The following are some suggestions for things to bring back as keepsakes from these locations:

Limoncello
Limoncello is a liqueur made from lemons, and Sorrento is famous for its lemons. It is a great way to taste the flavors of Sorrento and is a well-liked memento.

Sandals in Caprese
Handmade sandals that are both stylish and comfortable are Capri's specialty. You can choose the one that best suits your taste because they come in a variety of styles and colors.

Ceramics
Both Sorrento and Capri have a rich history of earthenware production, and you can track down various bright and mind-boggling pieces, like plates, containers, and tiles.

Woodwork with inlays

The intricate inlaid woodwork that can be found in Sorrento is well-known. The designs are created by cutting and joining various kinds of wood together. Furniture, frames, and jewelry boxes are among the many items available.

Perfumes
Capri perfumes are well-known for their distinctive scents and natural ingredients. There are citrus, floral, and woody notes among the scents.

Olive oil
Olive oil of excellent quality is produced in the area surrounding Sorrento, making it an excellent gift for foodies. Olive oil comes in a variety of forms, including extra-virgin, flavored, and infused oils.

Capri shorts
Capri pants are a sort of ladies' jeans that began in Capri. They're beautiful and snazzy, and you can track down them in various textures and varieties.

Coral ornaments
Sorrento and Capri are both known for their coral gems, which are produced using the coral that fills in the close by waters. Necklaces, bracelets, and earrings are among the many items available.

In general, Sorrento and Capri provide a diverse selection of mementos that are representative of the local customs and culture. Whether you're searching for something to wear, to adorn your home, or to enjoy, you're certain to find something that will help you to remember your excursion.

CHAPTER 15: SICILY

Sicily is the largest island in the Mediterranean Sea and is located just off Italy's southern coast. It is well-known for its breathtaking natural beauty, illustrious history, and vibrant culture. Throughout history, Sicily has been inhabited by many civilizations such as the Greeks, Romans, Arabs, and Normans. As a result, the island has a diverse cultural legacy, which is reflected in its architecture, art, and cuisine.

The ancient Greek city of Syracuse, the exquisite Baroque architecture of Noto, the Valley of the Temples in Agrigento, and the lovely beaches and nature reserves such as Zingaro Natural Reserve and Vendicari Natural Reserve are among the most popular attractions in Sicily. Sicily is also famous for its delectable cuisine, which includes regional specialties like arancini, caponata, and cannoli.

Sicily is a wonderful island in the Mediterranean Ocean and there are a lot of activities and see there. Here are a few ideas:

Agrigento's ancient ruins
This stunning collection of Greek temples and other ruins is one of Sicily's most important archaeological sites.

Visit Mount Etna
This dynamic spring of gushing lava is the most elevated in Europe and offers amazing perspectives from the top. You can take a directed climb, go skiing in winter, or Visit the magma fields.

Enjoy the seashores
Cefalù, San Vito lo Capo, and Taormina beaches are just a few of Sicily's many stunning beaches. Enjoy a swim in the turquoise waters, unwind on the white sands, or engage in water sports.

Go to Palermo
Sicily's capital is a lively and bustling city with a long history and culture. Take in the historic center, the markets, and some of Sicily's delectable cuisine.

Take a trip to the Aeolian Islands
These seven islands have stunning natural beauty and are off the coast of Sicily. Visit the dark sand sea shores, swim in the clear waters, and Visit the volcanic scenes.

Take a tour of the Temple Valley
Near Agrigento, this UNESCO World Heritage site has some of the most impressive ancient Greek ruins in the world.

Try some of the local food

Fresh seafood, pasta dishes, and sweet desserts are among the most popular dishes in Sicilian cuisine. Caponata, arancini, and cannoli are just a few of the local favorites.

Take a trip to the towns built in the Baroque period
Noto, Ragusa, and Modica are just a few of Sicily's most stunning Baroque towns. Admire the elaborate public squares, palaces, and churches.

Go wine sampling
Nero d'Avola, Cerasuolo di Vittoria, and Etna Rosso are three excellent wines from Sicily. Taste some of the region's wines at a winery.

In general, Sicily offers a rich social legacy, dazzling normal excellence, heavenly cooking, and a lot of outside exercises. Sicily has something for everyone, whether you're interested in history, art, food, nature, or both.

Where to stay in Sicily

In Sicily, you can choose from a wide range of accommodations to fit your needs and budget. Some popular choices are:

Hotels
Sicily has a wide selection of hotels, from budget-friendly establishments to luxurious ones. You can browse chain inns or store lodgings, contingent upon your requirements.

B&Bs
In Sicily, bed and breakfasts are a popular choice, especially if you want a more intimate stay. B&Bs can be found in both urban and rural areas.

Villas and Studios

Renting an apartment or villa can be a good choice if you are traveling with a group or intend to stay for a long time. Check on sites like Airbnb and Vrbo for a wide range of options.

Agriturismos
Sicily's agriturismos are farm stays that give guests a unique look at life in the country. You can take cooking classes or go on a farm tour, eat local food and drink, and stay on a working farm.

Hostels
Hostels are a great place to stay if you're traveling on a budget. There are numerous hostels in major Sicilian cities like Catania and Palermo.

Especially during the peak travel season, it is always a good idea to book your lodging in advance. Think about your budget, area inclinations, and the kind of involvement you need to have while picking your accommodation in Sicily.

Where to eat in Sicily

The Mediterranean Sea, Sicily's fertile land, and the many cultural influences that have shaped its history are the inspirations for its delicious and distinctive cuisine. Here are a few ideas for spots to eat in Sicily:

Trattoria da Enzo (Taormina)
This trattoria, run by a family, serves homemade pasta, fresh seafood, and delectable desserts in the picturesque town of Taormina.

Palermo's Osteria dei Vespri
Traditional Sicilian cuisine is modernized at this elegant restaurant in Palermo's center. Fresh fish, meat, and vegetables are just a few of the local products on their menu.

La Cambusa
Fresh fish, shellfish, and grilled octopus are among the many seafood options on the extensive menu at this charming restaurant in Cefalù, a coastal town.

Catania's I Banchi
This provincial restaurant in the memorable focus of Catania has practical experience in conventional Sicilian dishes made with new, occasional fixings.

Palermo's Antica Focacceria San Francesco
Famous for its Palermitan street food, such as arancini (fried rice balls), panelle (chickpea fritters), and sfincione (Sicilian pizza), this historic restaurant was established in 1834.

A Putia delle Cose Buone (Syracuse)
The authentic Sicilian cuisine that is served at this cozy trattoria in the heart of Syracuse is made with organic and locally sourced

ingredients. Some of the dishes include homemade pasta, grilled meats, and fresh vegetables.

Duomo's Restaurant (Ragusa)
This Michelin-starred restaurant, which is in the charming town of Ragusa, offers a modern take on Sicilian cuisine with dishes that use local ingredients like ricotta cheese, honey, and almonds.

What to bring home from Sicily

Sicily is a great place to buy souvenirs due to its stunning natural beauty, rich history, and culture. The following are some well-liked things that you might want to bring back from Sicily:

Products grown locally
Olive oil, sun-dried tomatoes, wine, chocolate, and honey are just a few of Sicily's delectable culinary offerings. Farms, food stores, and local markets all carry these items.

Ceramics
Ceramics from Sicily are well-known for their vibrant and intricate designs. They are available at local markets or pottery shops, and you can use them as a functional or pretty home accessory.

Handcrafted Lace
Sicilian trim is another famous keepsake that you can track down in the island's business sectors. The hand-made lacework is renowned for its exquisite design and high quality.

Puppets
Puppetry from Sicily is a well-established form of entertainment that originated in the Middle Ages. Local shops sell exquisitely crafted puppets, which are one-of-a-kind and memorable keepsakes.

Coral ornaments
Sicily is home to some of the world's most stunning coral reefs, and local shops sell stunning jewelry made from coral.

Products made from almonds
Almonds from Sicily are used to make a variety of goods, including marzipan, nougat, and almond milk. These items can be purchased at food stores or markets in your area.

T-shirts and bags as keepsakes
U-You can find many shops selling shirts and packs with Sicilian themes or logos, which make a tomfoolery and functional keepsake to bring back.

Keep in mind that when you shop in Sicily, it is always a good idea to look for products that are made locally to help the local economy and get a true Sicilian experience.

Sardinia is an Italian island in the Mediterranean Sea famed for its beautiful beaches, clear waters, and rough mountain scenery. It is the Mediterranean's second-largest island after Sicily and a famous tourist destination. The Costa Smeralda, a length of coastline famed for its stunning beaches and turquoise waters, is one of Sardinia's most famous attractions. Swimming, sunbathing, and water sports such as snorkeling and diving are available to visitors. Sardinia is also well-known for its delectable cuisine, which includes regional delicacies like pane carasau (a thin, crispy bread), culurgiones (a sort of pasta filled with potato and cheese), and roasted suckling pig. Visitors can also sample the island's well-known wines, like Cannonau and Vermentino.

What to do in Sardinia

The beautiful island of Sardinia is in the Mediterranean Sea, west of the Italian peninsula. Visitors can take advantage of a wide range of activities and attractions there. Here are a few things you can do in Sardinia:

Go to the beach
Sardinia is renowned for its delightful sea shores with clear water and white sand. The absolute most famous seashores include Spiaggia del Principe, Cala Luna, and Costa Smeralda.

Visit the Nuragic ruins
Numerous Nuragic ruins, which are megalithic structures from the Bronze Age, can be found in Sardinia. The most renowned Nuragic site is Su Nuraxi in Barumini.

Take a hike
Numerous hiking trails in Sardinia provide breathtaking views of the coastline and mountains. Probably the best paths include the Selvaggio Blu, the Supramonte, and the Gola su Gorropu.

Visit Cagliari, the country's capital
Cagliari is a beguiling city with a rich history and culture. The National Archaeological Museum, the Cathedral of Santa Maria, and the Castello di San Michele are among the must-see attractions.

Explore the regional cuisine
The cuisine of Sardinia is one of a kind and heavily influenced by its history and geography. The porceddu (roasted suckling pig), culurgiones (stuffed pasta), and seadas (a dessert made with cheese and honey) are among the must-try dishes.

Try some wine
Winemaking has a long history in Sardinia, and several wineries offer tours and tastings. Cannonau, Vermentino, and Carignano are among the most well-known Sardinian wines.

Visit the Maddalena Archipelago

Boating, snorkeling, and diving are some of the most popular activities on this group of islands off the coast of Sardinia. The islands are known for their clear waters and bountiful marine life.

Go to a festival in the area
The Sant'Efisio procession in Cagliari, the Redentore festival in Nuoro, and the Carnival of Mamoiada are just a few of the many traditional festivals that take place throughout the year in Sardinia. The island's culture and customs can only be experienced at these festivals.

Where to stay in Sardinia

Hotels
There are numerous hotels in Sardinia, ranging from budget-friendly options to luxurious resorts. The Costa Smeralda region is home to some of Sardinia's most opulent hotels.

B&Bs
In Sardinia, especially in the smaller towns and villages, bed and breakfasts are a popular option offering a range of accommodations to suit different budgets and tastes. Some popular B&Bs in Sardinia include Alba Rosa Bed & Breakfast, B&B Sa dom'e Forru, Casa Marina, B&B La Terrazza sul Mare, and B&B Sa Contissa.

Agriturismi
Numerous farms in Sardinia provide lodging for tourists. Traditional Sardinian life and cuisine can be experienced at agriturismi, which are typically found in rural areas.

Villas and studios
Renting an apartment or villa can be a good choice if you want to stay in Sardinia for a longer period or are traveling with a group. In comparison to staying in a hotel, this provides you with more flexibility and space and may be less expensive.

Camping

There are a lot of campgrounds in Sardinia, from simple camping spots to more expensive glamping options. Camping is a great way to see Sardinia's stunning natural beauty.

To ensure that you have the best possible time in Sardinia, make sure to do your homework and book your accommodation in advance.

Where to eat in Sardinia

Fresh seafood, pasta, bread, and a variety of meat dishes are just a few of Sardinia's distinctive and flavorful dishes. Here are a few prescribed eateries to have a go at during your visit to Sardinia:

Il Rifugio del Re

The Gulf of Arzachena can be seen from this restaurant, which is in the town of Arzachena. They spend significant time in new fish and Sardinian meats cooked on a wood-terminated barbecue. Attempt their particular dish, the lobster linguine.

Su Gologone

In the center of Sardinia, close to the town of Oliena, is this restaurant. It serves homemade pasta, roasted meats, and desserts made from scratch, all made with local ingredients, in the traditional Sardinian cuisine. They have a wide range of local wines, so it's worth checking out their wine selection as well.

The Li Tre Bicchi Farm

This ranch to-table café, situated in the field close to the town of Alghero, serves customary Sardinian cooking made with fixings obtained from their homestead. Their fixed-price menu changes daily as per season.

The Riccardo's Restaurant

In the town of Sant'Antioco, this restaurant is known for its seafood dishes and homemade desserts. They offer an assortment of new fish dishes, as well as customary Sardinian pasta dishes.

The Lamparas

This seafood restaurant is in the town of Alghero and has a beautiful spot right on the water. They have some expertise in new fish dishes, including their unique dish of spaghetti with ocean imp.

Su Nuraxi's Restaurant

This restaurant serves traditional Sardinian cuisine with a focus on meat dishes. It is close to the ancient ruins of Su Nuraxi. They are especially known for their nursing pig and sheep dishes.

Restaurant La Saletta

This café, situated in the town of Iglesias, offers a comfortable air and serves customary Sardinian dishes made with new, nearby fixings. Seafood and meat dishes, as well as pasta made by hand, are on their menu.

In general, Sardinia has a long and illustrious culinary history that is well worth learning about, and these are just a few of the many choices you can choose from. Make sure to try some of the local specialties, like the stuffed pasta called culurgiones and the crispy Sardinian bread called pane carasau.

What to bring home from Sardinia

Sardinia is known for its novel and excellent items, so there are a lot of things you can bring back as trinkets or gifts for loved ones. Here are a few concepts:

Sardinian wines

Sardinia creates a few brilliant wines, especially the red wines produced using the Cannonau grape. Search for bottles from neighborhood wineries, for example, Argiolas or Bar di Santadi.

Serrano cheese

Pecorino sardo, a hard sheep's milk cheese, and casu marzu, a pungent cheese made with live maggots, are two delicious kinds of cheese from Sardinia. Before attempting to bring casu marzu home, you should be aware that it is prohibited in many nations.

Sardinian clothing

Sardinia's textiles, particularly the traditional woolen shawls known as "tessuti a mano," are well-known. In towns like Nule and Samugheo, look for items made by local artisans.

Sardinian pottery

Pottery has been made in Sardinia for a long time, and beautiful handmade ceramics can be found in many towns and villages. Search for pieces with conventional Sardinian plans, similar to the brilliant "caddinas" utilized for putting away water or wine.

Sweets from Sardinia

Sardinia has various tasty desserts, including "sebadas," a seared baked good loaded up with cheddar and sprinkled with honey, and "amaretti," almond treats frequently presented with a glass of new wine.

Olive oil from Sardinia

The Bosana and Nera di Gonnos varieties, in particular, are used to make some of the best olive oil in Sardinia. Find bottles made by local businesses like Frantoio Murru and Olio Salvatore.

Sardinian blades

Sardinia has a long practice of blade-making, and you can track down excellent hand-tailored blades in numerous towns and towns.

Look for knives with traditional Sardinian patterns like "resolza" or "pattada."

Sardinian salt
Sardinia creates top-notch ocean salt, especially from the town of Trapani. Buy "sale marino" bags from local businesses.

Sardinian adornments
Jewelry-making is a long-standing tradition in Sardinia, especially with coral and filigree work. In cities like Alghero and Carloforte, look for items made by local artisans.

Liquors from Sardinia
The sweet and herbal "mirto," made from myrtle berries, and the bitter "filu'e ferru," made from wild herbs and distilled in copper stills, are two examples of the many liqueurs that Sardinia produces.

Sardinian fish
On the off chance that you're going with a cooler or protected pack, consider bringing back a portion of Sardinia's phenomenal fish, such as bottarga (dried mullet roe) or new fish filets.

In general, Sardinia has an abundance of one-of-a-kind and top-notch items that make fantastic trinkets or gifts. For the most authentic experience, make sure to shop around and find items made by local producers and artisans.

The Cinque Terre is a stunning and one-of-a-kind stretch of shoreline on the Italian Riviera in the Liguria area. Cinque Terre translates as "Five Lands" and refers to the five magnificent coastal communities that comprise the area: Monterosso al Mare, Vernazza, Corniglia, Manarola, and Riomaggiore. The Cinque Terre is famous for its cliffs, colorful buildings, vineyards, and terraced hillsides that slope down to the sea. Visitors can explore the area on foot by following the famed hiking trail that connects the five towns, or by hopping on a train that connects them in a matter of minutes. Whether you enjoy hiking, going to the beach, or simply taking in the distinct ambiance of these magnificent coastal communities, the Cinque Terre is a must-visit destination.

What to do in the Clique Terre

Cinque Terre is a stunning stretch of coastline in Italy's Liguria that is renowned for its vibrant towns and picturesque landscapes. Here are what should be done in Cinque Terre:

Go to each of the five villages
Every village has its charm and personality:
- Vernazza: This village is renowned for its vibrant homes, lovely harbor, and historic castle.
- Monterosso al Mare: This is a sizable community with a lengthy sandy beach. It boasts a quaint old town with small, colorful buildings, restaurants, and many cafes.
- Riomaggiore: This is distinguished by its pastel-colored homes and steep, narrow streets. There are many hiking trails there that lead to beautiful vistas.
- Corniglia: This village provides breathtaking views of the surrounding area and is built on a mountaintop overlooking the sea. Corniglia is renowned for its small-town charm and serene, quiet atmosphere.
- Manarola: This village is renowned for its vibrant homes and lovely harbor. Various hiking trails lead to breathtaking vistas, as well as a little rocky beach.

Climb the Sentiero Azzurro paths
The Sentiero Azzurro, or Blue Trail, connects all five villages and is a popular hiking trail. The villages and coastline can be seen magnificently from the trail.

Take a break at the beach
The Cinque Terre's largest beach is in Monterosso al Mare; however, each village has its own beach or swimming area.

Explore the regional cuisine
Pesto sauce, focaccia bread, and seafood dishes are among Ligurian cuisine's most well-known dishes. Try them at one of the nearby eateries. Being a waterfront region, Cinque Terre is popular for its

new fish. Try local dishes like octopus salad, seafood risotto, and anchovies.

Take a tour by boat
To take in the stunning coastline from the water, you can take a boat tour from one village to the next.

Go to the wineries
The terraced vineyards of Cinque Terre, where grapes are grown on steep hillsides, are famous. You can tour the vineyards and try some of the region's wines.

Take in the sunset
From one of the villages' panoramic viewpoints, you can watch the sunset over the sea.

Visit the cultural sites
There are numerous museums, churches, and historic sites to explore in Cinque Terre, which has a rich culture and history. Visit the Church of San Lorenzo in Manarola or the Sanctuary of Nostra Signora di Reggio in Vernazza.

Swim in the natural pools
The Piscina Naturale in Corniglia and the Bay of Fegina in Monterosso are two natural swimming holes in the region.

Go diving or snorkeling
The waters of Cinque Terre are ideal for scuba diving and snorkeling. You can see beautiful fish, coral, and even wrecks.

Go to a neighborhood celebration
Cinque Terre has a few celebrations, for example, the Monterosso Lemon Celebration in May, the Fish Celebration in Riomaggiore in August, and the Grape Celebration in Manarola in September.

Attend a cooking lesson
In a cooking class, learn how to make focaccia and pesto, two typical Ligurian dishes. Tourists can take cooking classes at a number of the area's restaurants.

Visit close by towns
Cinque Terre is an extraordinary base to Visit different towns in the Liguria locale, like Portofino, Genoa, and St Nick Margherita Ligure.

Where to stay in the Clique Terre

The Cinque Terre is a famous traveler objective situated on the shore of Liguria, Italy. It involves five little beachfront towns, specifically Monterosso al Mare, Vernazza, Corniglia, Manarola, and Riomaggiore. There is an assortment of accommodation choices accessible in the Cinque Terre, from lavish hotels to budget inns. The following are some well-liked choices for lodging in the Cinque Terre:

Hotels
The Cinque Terre is home to several hotels, ranging from high-end establishments to budget-friendly options. The Hotel Porto Roca in Monterosso al Mare, the Hotel La Spiaggia in Riomaggiore, and the Hotel Al Terra di Mare in Levanto are all well-known hotels.

Hotels and inns
If you want to stay in the Cinque Terre and have a more intimate experience, bed and breakfasts are a great choice. Some famous overnight boardinghouses remember Affittacamere Le Giare for Vernazza and Da Paulin in Corniglia.

Lofts and Excursion Rentals
In the Cinque Terre, there are numerous vacation rentals and apartments that are ideal for groups or families traveling together.

A few famous choices remember Condo for Manarola and Cinque Terre Extravagance Loft in Riomaggiore.

Hostels
In the Cinque Terre, there are numerous hostels for travelers on a tight budget. A few well-known choices remember Ostello Tramonti for Biassa and La Francesca Lodging in Bonassola.

While picking accommodation in the Cinque Terre, it's essential to consider factors like area, accommodations, and cost. Additionally, it's a good idea to reserve your lodging in advance, especially during the summer and fall.

Where to eat in the Clique Terre

Cinque Terre is a lovely region in Italy, known for its breathtaking shoreline and beautiful towns. The following are some recommendations for excellent eateries in Cinque Terre:

Trattoria dal Billy
In Manarola, Trattoria dal Billy is a restaurant known for its delicious seafood and stunning sea views.

Ristorante Miky
This café offers a wide choice of conventional Ligurian dishes made with new, privately obtained fixings.

Il Pirata delle Cinque Terre
Situated in Vernazza, this comfortable café works with fish and offers some amazing vegan choices.

Osteria Baracco
This is a charming restaurant that serves delicious homemade pasta and a wide range of regional wines.

Ristorante Belforte

This is a restaurant in the picturesque village of Vernazza that serves excellent seafood and has stunning views of the sea.

San Martino Gastronomia

This is a small, family-owned restaurant in Riomaggiore that is famous for its homemade, fresh pasta and other traditional Ligurian dishes.

Il Grottino

This eatery offers a comfortable and heartfelt environment with staggering perspectives on the town and the ocean. Their fish dishes are enthusiastically suggested.

Trattoria Da Oscar

In Corniglia, Trattoria Da Oscar is a trattoria that serves delicious homemade food, including a variety of seafood dishes, in a welcoming setting.

Enoteca da Eliseo

This is a wine bar and restaurant in Vernazza that serves delicious traditional Ligurian fare and a wide selection of wines from the region.

Il Ciliegio

In Monterosso, there is a restaurant called Il Ciliegio that has a warm atmosphere and a great selection of homemade pasta, seafood, and other Ligurian specialties.

Try some of the local wines, such as Sciacchetrà, a sweet wine made in the area, at any restaurant you choose. Additionally, gelato, which is a Cinque Terre must-have, should not be missed!

What to bring home from the Clique Terre

Here are some ideas for Cinque Terre-related gifts and mementos to take home with you:

Local Wine
Cinque Terre is known for its delicious wines, especially the white Sciacchetrà, which is made through a special method. You can track down containers of this wine at neighborhood shops and wineries.

Pesto
The basil utilized in making Pesto alla Genovese is filled in Liguria, which is the locale where Cinque Terre is found. Pesto jars are available for purchase and make excellent gifts or keepsakes.

Ceramics
Ceramics and pottery made by hand can be found in the local shops of the Cinque Terre villages. Bright colors and conventional patterns are frequently used to decorate the pieces.

Olive oil
Olive oil is a staple in Italian cooking, and you can find top-notch olive oil produced using nearby olives in Cinque Terre. Olive oil bottles with the labels "olio di oliva" or "olio extravergine di oliva" are your best bet.

Limoncino
This liqueur has a lemon flavor and is popular in Cinque Terre and the area around it. Local wineries and shops sell bottles of limoncino.

Local honey
There are a lot of bees in Cinque Terre, and the honey that is made there is delicious. Honey jars marked "miele" should be looked for.

Anchovies

The local cuisine relies heavily on anchovies, which can be found salted or in oil-packed jars in local stores. They make for an exceptional and delectable trinket.

.

CHAPTER 18: THE DOLOMITES

The Dolomites are a magnificent mountain range in northeastern Italy's Trentino-Alto Adige/Südtirol region. The Southern Limestone Alps, which are recognized for their spectacular peaks, picturesque valleys, and rich cultural legacy are part of the Dolomites. The Dolomites are a popular outdoor recreation destination, with activities such as hiking, mountain biking, rock climbing, skiing, and snowboarding available. The area contains a network of well-marked paths that range from simple treks to difficult mountain climbs. Visitors may experience world-class skiing and snowboarding in the winter, with many resorts providing sophisticated facilities and services.

In addition to their natural splendor, the Dolomites have a rich cultural legacy, with several attractive towns and villages dotting the valleys and hillsides. Many of these towns have a strong hospitality tradition, with local hotels and restaurants serving authentic cuisine and warm hospitality.

The Dolomites, a mountain range in northeastern Italy, are home to a variety of outdoor pursuits and breathtaking scenery. Here are a few ideas for what to do in the Dolomites:

Hiking
There are a lot of beautiful hiking trails in the Dolomites, from easy strolls to strenuous treks. The Seceda Panorama Trail, the Alta Via 1 loop, and the Tre Cime di Lavaredo route are all well-known routes.

Skiing
Numerous ski resorts in the Dolomites offer downhill and cross-country skiing, snowboarding, and other snow-related activities. The Dolomites are a popular destination for winter sports.

Climbing rocks
The steep limestone cliffs of the Dolomites are well-known and provide numerous challenging rock climbing routes. Some famous climbing regions include the Tre Cime di Lavaredo, the Sella Gathering, and the Civetta.

Via ferrata routes
Via ferrata routes is an exciting way to see the Dolomites for people who want to do both hiking and climbing at the same time. These safeguarded ascending courses include steel links and stepping stools to support rising.

Cycling
For cyclists of all skill levels, the Dolomites offer numerous scenic on- and off-road cycling routes.

Natural life spotting

Ibex, chamois, marmots, and eagles are among the many species of wildlife that call the Dolomites their home. Take a tour with a guide to learn more about these creatures and the places where they live.

Taking a spa break
Following a lot of time climbing, climbing, or skiing, loosen up in one of the Dolomites' numerous spas, which offer a scope of health medicines and offices.

Visits to museums
There are numerous picturesque towns and villages, as well as museums and art galleries, to explore in the Dolomites, which are also full of culture and history.

In general, the Dolomites have a wide range of experiences and activities for visitors of all kinds.

Where to stay in the Dolomites

There are a lot of accommodation choices accessible in the Dolomites to suit different budgets and inclinations. It's ideal to book ahead of time, particularly during peak season (December to February for skiing, and June to September for climbing).

Refugios
Hikers and climbers frequently make use of these high-altitude mountain huts as places to rest and sleep. They are typically inexpensive, basic, and simple, but they can provide stunning views and a true mountain experience. The popular refugios Rifugio Lagazuoi, Rifugio Averau, and Rifugio Scoiattoli are all located in the Dolomites.

Hotels and inns
These are typically family-owned businesses that provide a more personal and intimate setting. The B&Bs Garni Iosc in Ortisei, Ciasa

Amalia in San Cassiano, and Villa La Bercia in Cortina d'Ampezzo are among the region's most well-liked bed and breakfasts.

Chalets and apartments

In the Dolomites, several apartments and chalets can be rented for people who want a little bit more privacy and space. These can be as small studio apartments as they are large chalets that can hold multiple people. Dolomite Mountains and Dolomites Chalet are two well-known rental companies.

Camping

Camping enthusiasts can find affordable lodging in the Dolomites at several campsites scattered throughout the region. Camping Sass Dlacia in Corvara, Camping Al Plan in San Vigilio di Marebbe, and Camping Val di Sole in Val di Sole are all well-liked camping grounds.

It's important to remember that the Dolomites are a popular destination, especially during the peak season. To avoid disappointment, it's best to book lodging in advance. Also, numerous facilities offer comprehensive bundles that include exercises like climbing or skiing, so make certain to check for any exceptional offers that might be accessible.

Where to eat in the Dolomites

From traditional, hearty mountain cuisine to refined gourmet dishes, the Dolomites offer a wide range of culinary experiences. Here are a few proposals for spots to eat in the Dolomites:

The Fuciade Refuge

Situated in the San Pellegrino Pass, this mountain cottage offers a wonderful perspective on the encompassing mountains and serves conventional dishes, for example, venison stew, hand-crafted pasta, and polenta.

Tivoli Restaurant

This Michelin-featured café in Cortina d'Ampezzo serves imaginative dishes with an emphasis on neighborhood fixings, like mountain spices, berries, and wild game.

The Lagazuoi Refuge

Situated at 2,752 meters on the Lagazuoi mountain, this mountain cabin offers stunning perspectives on the Dolomites and serves conventional dishes, for example, grain soup, dumplings, and apple strudel.

Ristorante El Molin

This café in the town of San Cassiano serves a combination of Italian and Tyrolean cooking, with dishes, for example, meat carpaccio with truffle oil, pumpkin ravioli, and apple strudel.

Baita Checco

This rustic mountain hut, which is in the Alta Badia ski area, serves traditional dishes like goulash soup, speck and cheese platters, and homemade apple strudel.

Restaurant in St. Michael

In Corvara, this Michelin-starred restaurant serves gourmet fare like lobster risotto, foie gras terrine, and venison with wild berries.

Rifugio Scoiattoli

Situated at the foot of the Tofana di Rozes mountain, this mountain cottage offers an all-encompassing perspective on the Dolomites and serves conventional dishes like polenta, wieners, and apple strudel.

The Dolomites are home to a plethora of excellent eateries, just a few of which can be found here. For authentic regional cuisine, you should also check out the local trattorias, osterias, and agriturismi.

From traditional, hearty mountain cuisine to refined gourmet dishes, the Dolomites offer a wide range of culinary experiences. Here are a few proposals for spots to eat in the Dolomites:

The Fuciade Refuge
Situated in the San Pellegrino Pass, this mountain cottage offers a wonderful perspective on the encompassing mountains and serves conventional dishes, for example, venison stew, hand-crafted pasta, and polenta.

Tivoli Restaurant
This Michelin-featured café in Cortina d'Ampezzo serves imaginative dishes with an emphasis on neighborhood fixings, like mountain spices, berries, and wild game.

The Lagazuoi Refuge
Situated at 2,752 meters on the Lagazuoi mountain, this mountain cabin offers stunning perspectives on the Dolomites and serves conventional dishes, for example, grain soup, dumplings, and apple strudel.

El Molin's Restaurant
This café in the town of San Cassiano serves a combination of Italian and Tyrolean cooking, with dishes, for example, meat carpaccio with truffle oil, pumpkin ravioli, and apple strudel.

The Baita Checco Restaurant
This rustic mountain hut, which is in the Alta Badia ski area, serves traditional dishes like goulash soup, speck and cheese platters, and homemade apple strudel.

Restaurant in St. Michael

In Corvara, this Michelin-starred restaurant serves gourmet fare like lobster risotto, foie gras terrine, and venison with wild berries.

Rifugio Scoiattoli
Situated at the foot of the Tofana di Rozes mountain, this mountain cottage offers an all-encompassing perspective on the Dolomites and serves conventional dishes like polenta, wieners, and apple strudel.

The Dolomites are home to a plethora of excellent eateries, just a few of which can be found here. For authentic regional cuisine, you should also check out the local trattorias, osterias, and agriturismi.

CHAPTER 19: THE ITALIAN LAKES

Italy is home to the absolute most breathtaking lakes in Europe, which are famous objections for travelers and local people the same. The following are some of Italy's most well-known lakes:

Lake Como
The picturesque villages, stunning villas, and dramatic mountain backdrop of Lake Como, which is in Lombardy, are what make it so popular. It is a great place for water sports and hiking, as well as a popular destination for celebrities and wealthy tourists.

Lake Garda
Lake Garda, the largest lake in Italy, is a popular tourist destination in Northern Italy. It is surrounded by charming towns and villages, and there are numerous outdoor pursuits to enjoy, such as water sports, cycling, and hiking.

Lake Maggiore

Lake Maggiore is famous for its stunning islands, including Isola Bella and Isola Madre. It is on the border of Switzerland and Italy. Additionally, the lake is surrounded by charming towns and villages, making it an excellent location for exploration.

Lake Isleo
Lake Iseo, which is in Lombardy and is smaller than the other lakes on this list, is famous for its clear water and beautiful views. Numerous charming towns in the vicinity can be explored, and it is a popular location for cycling and hiking.

Lake Orta
This is a small, picturesque lake in the Piedmont that tourists frequently overlook. It is surrounded by charming towns and villages, including Orta San Giulio, a medieval town, and the area has numerous hiking trails.

Lake Trasimeno
The largest lake in Central Italy is Lake Trasimeno, which can be found in Umbria. It is a popular spot for water sports, and the region is home to numerous charming towns and villages, including Castiglione del Lago, a medieval town.

Lake Bolsena
Situated in Lazio, Lake Bolsena is known for its clear waters and grand perspectives. It's a famous objective for swimming and water sports, and there are a lot of climbing trails nearby too.

Lake Bracciano
Lake Bracciano, which is just outside of Rome, is a popular day trip from the city. It's encircled by beguiling towns and towns, and there are a lot of outside exercises to appreciate, including climbing and cruising.

Italy's coastline is renowned for its stunning beaches and crystal-clear waters. On your coast-to-coast trip through Italy, here are some of the best beaches to check out:

Spiaggia dei Conigli (Lampedusa)
Every year, this stunning beach on the Sicilian island of Lampedusa is named one of Italy's best. It is a must-visit location for beach lovers thanks to its crystal-clear turquoise waters and white sand.

Cala Mariolu (Sardinia)
Situated on the east shore of Sardinia, Cala Mariolu is a segregated ocean side open exclusively by boat. The water at the beach is crystal clear, the marine life is colorful, and the scenery is breathtaking.

Porto Giunco (Southwestern Sardinia)
This beach has soft, white sand and clear, blue water. It is in the middle of the Mediterranean. It is encircled by lavish plant life and is an extraordinary spot for swimming, sunbathing, and unwinding.

Spiaggia del Fornillo (Positano)
In Positano, this stunning beach is away from the bustle of the main town. It has stunning views of the coastline and waters that are ideal for swimming that are crystal clear.

Baia dei Turchi (Salento)
This wonderful ocean side on the Adriatic bank of Salento offers completely clear waters and fine white sand. Because it is surrounded by lush Mediterranean vegetation, it is the ideal location for nature enthusiasts.

Isola Bella (Taormina)

This lovely oceanside in Taormina, Sicily is encircled by completely clear waters and offers breathtaking perspectives on the shore. It is accessible by a precarious flight of stairs and is a must-visit for ocean-side darlings.

Tropea (Southern Calabria)
The waters at this picturesque beach in the southern part of Calabria are crystal clear, and the view of the old town is stunning. It is a popular spot to enjoy the Italian coast by swimming, sunbathing, and other activities.

Spiaggia La Pelosa (Sardinia)
This breathtaking ocean side is situated on the northwest shore of Sardinia and is known for its unmistakable turquoise waters and delicate white sand. Because it is one of Sardinia's most popular beaches, it can get crowded during the summer.

Arienzo Beach (Praiano)
The Amalfi Coast's picturesque beach has stunning views of the coastline and clear water. It's a great spot for swimming and unwinding in a small fishing village. Arienzo Beach is a tiny, undeveloped beach that lies close to Praiano. It is a pebble beach with crystal-clear waves and breathtaking ocean views.

Cala Goloritzè (Sardis)
This little ocean side on the east shoreline of Sardinia is open simply by boat or a long climb. It is encircled by precipices and offers clear waters and dazzling perspectives.

Paraggi Beach (Liguria)
This little town on the Ligurian coast is known for its bright structures and lovely seashores. It has stunning views, crystal-clear water, and a tranquil atmosphere. Paraggi Beach is a stunning and well-liked beach that is conveniently close to Portofino. It is a tiny

pebble beach with beautiful waters and breathtaking views of the hills in the distance.

Fegina Beach and Old Town Beach (Monterosso al Mare)
The vibrant buildings and stunning beaches of this little town on the Italian Riviera are well-known. Fegina Beach is wonderful for swimming, sunbathing, and taking in the breathtaking views of the coastline. The beach is surrounded by eateries, cafes, and bars, making it a wonderful area to unwind and partake in some food and beverages. The Old Town Beach is more private and intimate, with beautiful seas and breathtaking cliff views. It's a nice location to get away from the crowds and relax.

Marina Piccola Beach (Capri)
The waters at this small Capri beach are crystal clear, and the views of the coastline are breathtaking. It is a must-see for beach lovers and can only be reached by boat or via a strenuous hike.

San Vito lo Capo (Sicily)
The soft, white sand and crystal-clear waters of this stunning beach in western Sicily are to die for. It is a popular spot to swim, sunbathe, and enjoy the Italian coast because it is surrounded by mountains. It is considered one of the best beaches in Italy!

CHAPTER 21: THE BEST FOOD TO EAT

The best way to learn about Italian culture is through its food, and Italy is known for its mouthwatering cuisine. Italy's culinary landscape is one-of-a-kind and diverse due to its diverse regions and long history. Italy has a wide variety of mouthwatering dishes to try, including hearty pasta dishes from Tuscany and fresh seafood from the Amalfi Coast. Italy is a foodie's paradise because it has so many delicious dishes and flavors to entice your taste buds. Italian cuisine has something for everyone, from the classic pasta dishes of Rome to Sicilian seafood delights. The following are some of Italy's best dishes:

Pizza

No trip to Italy would be complete without a slice. Naples is the home of the first pizza, so make certain to attempt the exemplary Margherita, which comprises pureed tomatoes, mozzarella cheddar, and basil leaves. You can also try the marinara, which has tomato and garlic on top, or the quattro formaggi, which is a pizza with four different kinds of cheese.

Pasta

Pasta is another staple of Italian cuisine that can be found in many different flavors and shapes. A traditional Roman dish is a carbonara, which is made with cheese, bacon, and egg yolks. On the off chance that you are in Bologna, make certain to attempt the tagliatelle al ragù, a pasta dish made with a rich meat sauce. In southern Italy, you can appreciate pasta alla norma, which is a pasta dish with eggplant, pureed tomatoes, and ricotta cheddar.

Gelato

Gelato is Italy's take on ice cream, but it's creamier and lower in fat. It is made with natural ingredients like chocolate, fruit, and fresh milk. Try the stracciatella, hazelnut, and pistachio flavors.

Fish

Italy's longshore implies that fish is a noticeable component of the nation's cooking. You can savor a variety of seafood dishes in Sicily, including spaghetti alle vongole, which is made with clams and garlic, and pesce spada alla ghiotta, which is a swordfish dish that is made with tomatoes, olives, and capers. If you're in Venice, you should try the traditional risotto ai frutti di mare, a risotto with a variety of seafood.

Truffles

The underground fungus known as truffle is renowned throughout Italy. They're used in a lot of dishes and have a strong, earthy flavor. Try truffle pasta, a straightforward pasta dish made with butter and shaved truffles. Alternatively, you can savor a truffle risotto, or pizza.

Tiramisu

This exemplary Italian treat is made with ladyfingers plunged into coffee and layered with a combination of mascarpone cheddar, sugar, and egg yolks. After that, cocoa powder is applied to it. Tiramisu was first made in Veneto, but it is now popular all over Italy.

Wine

Italy is one of the world's top winemakers, and there is a wine to suit each sense of taste. Make sure to try the Barolo, a red wine from Piedmont, or the Chianti, a red wine from Tuscany. Try the white wine from Veneto called Soave if you like white wine.

Prosciutto and Cheese

Prosciutto is a must-try item when visiting Italy, which is known for its delicious cured meats and cheeses. Other cured meats, such as salami, and a variety of cheeses, such as Parmigiano Reggiano or pecorino, are frequently paired with this dry-cured ham. Make sure to serve it with some freshly baked bread and red wine.

Osso Buco

Osso Buco is a traditional Milanese dish made with braised veal shanks, vegetables, white wine, and broth. Scooping out the bone's marrow and mixing it with the sauce gives it a rich and savory flavor. Typically, it is accompanied by polenta or saffron risotto.

Cannoli

Cannoli is a Sicilian pastry in the shape of a tube that is stuffed with sweetened ricotta cheese and chocolate chips, candied fruit, or nuts. The cake shell is firm and crunchy, while the filling is rich and liberal. After a seafood feast in Sicily, this dessert is perfect.

Focaccia

Focaccia is a type of flatbread that is a staple in many parts of Italy. It comes in flavors like rosemary, garlic, or tomato. It is much of the time filled in as an hors d'oeuvre or bite, and you might find it loaded down with cheddar or different fixings. Focaccia is great as a quick snack, picnic lunch, or on the go.

Bistecca alla Fiorentina

Bistecca alla Fiorentina is a specialty of Tuscany that is typically made from Chianina cattle, an Italian breed of cattle. It is a thick, juicy steak. After being seasoned with olive oil, salt, and pepper, it is grilled over a wood fire. It is grilled to perfection and can be divided among various individuals because of its huge size.

Aperitivo

The pre-dinner drink known as an aperitivo is typically served with chips, cheese, olives, or other small snacks. In Italy, people gather for a drink and nibbles before dinner as a popular social activity. Aperol spritz, Campari, and Negroni are some popular aperitivo drinks.

There are many different types of Italian food, and each region has its specialties and flavors. Italy has something for everyone, whether you like pasta, pizza, seafood, meat dishes, or both.

Italy is a lovely country with a rich history, tasty food, and a fabulous landscape. If you're thinking about going to Italy, here are some things to keep in mind:

When to Visit Italy
While Italy is a stunning destination year-round, the best time to go will largely depend on what you hope to do and see while you're there.

Italy is best visited in the spring (April to June) or fall (September to November) if you want to explore the cities, go to museums and historical sites, or eat local food. The summer months (June to August) are the finest times to travel to Italy if you want to explore the beaches and coastal towns. The greatest time to travel to Italy if you enjoy winter sports like skiing and snowboarding is from December through February.

How to get to Italy
● By Plane: The majority of international visitors land in Italy by plane. Italy has numerous airports, including those in Rome, Milan, Florence, Venice, and Naples, to name a few.
● By Train: You can ride a train to Italy if you're coming from another European nation such as Paris, Geneva, and Vienna, among others.
● By car: You can drive to Italy if you're coming from another European nation. A network of motorways connects Italy to other European nations, and most large cities offer vehicle rentals.
● By ferry: You can travel to Italy by ferry from Greece, Spain, or North Africa.

Requirements for entry

Before you go, find out what the current entry requirements are for Italy. A valid passport or visa may be required, depending on your nationality. A negative COVID-19 test result or proof of vaccination may also be required.

Currency
The euro is Italy's official currency. Because not all establishments accept credit cards, you should always have some cash on hand, especially for smaller purchases.

Language
Italy uses Italian as its official language. Even though a lot of people in Italy speak English, you should learn a few basic Italian phrases to help you communicate with the locals.

Transport
The trains, buses, and metros that makeup Italy's public transportation system are all of the highest quality. To save time and money, you might want to buy a pass or ticket in advance.

Accommodation
Italy has an extensive variety of accommodation choices, including lodgings, overnight boardinghouses, and getaway rentals. Search for facilities that are centrally situated to get a good deal on transportation.

Food
Pizza, pasta, and wine are some of the best things about Italian food. Try local delicacies, but remember that every region has its distinct cuisine.

Tipping
Although it is not required, tipping is appreciated for excellent service in Italy. In restaurants, a 10% tip is common, but check your bill because some may already have a service charge included.

Safety
Although Italy is generally safe, you should always be aware of your surroundings, especially in tourist areas where pickpocketing can occur.

Weather
Italy has warm summers and mild winters thanks to its Mediterranean climate. Check the weather forecast before you go so that you can be ready for it.

Vacation destinations
Ancient ruins, museums, and art galleries are just a few of Italy's cultural and historical attractions. To save time and avoid long lines, you might want to consider purchasing tickets in advance.

Classic Italy Itinerary

Day 1-2: Rome

Visit the Colosseum, the Roman Forum, the Pantheon, and the Vatican City

Day 3-4: Florence

Visit the Duomo, Uffizi Gallery, and Ponte Vecchio

Day 5-6: Venice

Take a gondola ride and visit St. Mark's Basilica and Doge's Palace

Day 7-8: Cinque Terre

Hike the famous trail between the five colorful villages along the coast

Day 9-10: Amalfi Coast

Visit the picturesque towns of Positano, Amalfi, and Ravello

Art and Culture Itinerary

Day 1-3: Florence

Explore the city's art galleries and museums, including the Uffizi Gallery and the Accademia Gallery

Day 4-5: Pisa

Visit the Leaning Tower of Pisa and the Piazza dei Miracoli

Day 6-7: Siena

See the Piazza del Campo, the Palazzo Pubblico, and the Siena Cathedral

Day 8-9: Ravenna

Admire the stunning mosaics at the Basilica of San Vitale and the Mausoleum of Galla Placidia

Day 10-11: Rome

Explore the Vatican City and its museums, the Capitoline Museums, and the Borghese Gallery

Family-Friendly Itinerary

Day 1-3: Rome

Visit the Colosseum, the Roman Forum, the Pantheon, and the Vatican City

Day 4-5: Florence

Explore the city's art galleries and museums, including the Uffizi Gallery and the Accademia Gallery

Day 6-7: Venice

Take a gondola ride and visit St. Mark's Basilica and Doge's Palace

Day 8-9: Lake Como

Enjoy the scenic views and outdoor activities like hiking, boating, and swimming

Day 10-11: Gardaland

Visit the amusement park for a day of fun and thrills

Food and Wine Itinerary

Day 1-3: Bologna

Taste the famous Bolognese sauce and visit the food markets and factories

Day 4-5: Chianti Region

Explore the wineries and taste the Chianti Classico wine

Day 6-7: Naples

Try the authentic Neapolitan pizza and visit the local markets

Day 8-9: Sicily

Taste the local cuisine, including seafood, cannoli, and gelato

Day 10-11: Rome

Indulge in pasta, gelato, and other Italian specialties in the Eternal City

Romantic Itinerary

Day 1-3: Venice

Take a gondola ride and visit St. Mark's Basilica and Doge's Palace

Day 4-5: Verona

Visit the romantic city of Romeo and Juliet and see the balcony of Juliet's house

Day 6-7: Tuscany
Enjoy the picturesque countryside, wineries, and hot air balloon rides
Day 8-9: Amalfi Coast
Visit the picturesque towns of Positano, Amalfi, and Ravello
Day 10-11: Capri
Take a boat ride to the island and enjoy the scenic views, beaches, and romantic restaurants

Historical Itinerary:
Day 1-3: Rome
Visit the Colosseum, the Roman Forum, the Pantheon, and the Vatican City
Day 4-5: Pompeii
Explore the ancient city that was destroyed by the eruption of Mount Vesuvius
Day 6-7: Paestum
See the well-preserved Greek temples and ruins
Day 8-9: Matera
Visit the "Sassi" or cave dwellings that are over 9,000 years old
Day 10-11: Turin
Discover the city's history as the first capital of Italy and its connections to the Italian monarchy

Outdoor Adventure Itinerary
Day 1-3: Dolomites
Go hiking, rock climbing, and mountain biking in the stunning mountain range
Day 4-5: Lake Garda
Try windsurfing, kitesurfing, and sailing on the largest lake in Italy
Day 6-7: Tuscany
Go horseback riding or hot air ballooning over the picturesque countryside
Day 8-9: Cinque Terre

Hike the famous trail between the five colorful villages along the coast

Day 10-11: Sicily

Explore the stunning natural scenery of the island, including Mount Etna, the Aeolian Islands, and the Valley of the Temples

Budget-Friendly Itinerary

Day 1-3: Rome

Visit the free attractions like the Trevi Fountain, the Spanish Steps, and the Piazza Navona

Day 4-5: Naples

Visit the free attractions like the Piazza del Plebiscito and the Royal Palace of Naples

Day 6-7: Bari

Explore the historic city center and the free attractions like the Basilica of San Nicola and the Castello Normanno-Svevo

Day 8-9: Matera

Visit the free attractions like the Piazza Vittorio Veneto and the Sassi

Day 10-11: Florence

Visit the free attractions like the Piazza del Duomo, the Piazza della Signoria, and the Ponte Vecchio.

Art and Architecture Itinerary

Day 1-3: Florence

Visit the city's art museums and galleries, including the Uffizi Gallery and the Accademia Gallery

Day 4-5: Milan

See the iconic Cathedral of Milan and visit the Pinacoteca di Brera art museum

Day 6-7: Venice

Explore the city's architecture, including St. Mark's Basilica and the Doge's Palace

Day 8-9: Pisa

See the Leaning Tower of Pisa and other historic landmarks in the city center

Day 10-11: Rome
Visit the city's iconic monuments and buildings, including the Colosseum, the Roman Forum, and the Pantheon.

<u>Coastal Itinerary</u>
Day 1-3: Amalfi Coast
Enjoy the picturesque towns of Positano, Amalfi, and Ravello, and take a boat tour to see the coastline from the water

Day 4-5: Capri
Visit the island's beaches and the Blue Grotto, and take a chairlift to the top of Mount Solaro for stunning views

Day 6-7: Sicily
Visit the beautiful beaches of Taormina and the Aeolian Islands, and take a boat tour to see the stunning coastline

Day 8-9: Sardinia
Explore the island's beaches and visit the Maddalena Archipelago for a day trip

Day 10-11: Cinque Terre
Visit the picturesque towns of Riomaggiore, Manarola, Corniglia, Vernazza, and Monterosso al Mare, and hike the famous trail between them

CONCLUSIONS

Everyone who comes to Italy falls in love with the country. It is a one-of-a-kind and unforgettable destination due to its beauty, history, and culture. We trust this movement guide has given you all the data you really want to design your excursion and that you're currently anxious to encounter Italy's wizardry for yourself.

Be patient, immerse yourself in the local culture, and savor the delectable wine and food. Whether you're investigating the clamoring roads of Rome, cruising through the channels of Venice, or climbing through the staggering Dolomite Mountains, Italy vows to have an enduring impact on you. Therefore, prepare yourself for a once-in-a-lifetime adventure in the land of la dolce vita by packing your belongings.

INDEX

DEAR READER, I HOPE YOU ENJOYED MY GUIDE. PLEASE SCAN THE FOLLOWING TO READ 100+ SENTENCES AND THEIR ITALIAN TRANSLATION THAT ALL TRAVELERS NEED TO KNOW.

THANK U FOR YOUR PURCHASE!

SCAN ME

Made in the USA
Monee, IL
27 June 2023

37649565R00083